CAKES AND PASTRIES

GOOD HOUSEKEEPING
STEP-BY-STEP COOKERY

CAKES AND PASTRIES

GUILD PUBLISHING LONDON

This edition published 1987 by
Book Club Associates
by arrangement with Ebury Press

Consultant editor: Jeni Wright
Editors: Gill Edden, Felicity Jackson, Maria Mosby
Design by Roger Daniels
Drawings by Kate Simunek
Photographs by Paul Kemp

The Publishers would especially like to thank Jane Kemp and Divertimenti
for their help in providing accessories for photography.

Cover photograph: Rich Chocolate Cake (page 55) and Glazed Fruit Tarts
(page 107)

Filmset by Advanced Filmsetters (Glasgow) Ltd

Printed and bound in Spain by
Printer Industria Grafica S.A., Barcelona
D.L.B. 23742-1987

CONTENTS

COOKERY NOTES

Follow either metric or imperial measures for the recipes in this book as they are not interchangeable. Sets of spoon measures are available in both metric and imperial size to give accurate measurement of small quantities. All spoon measures are level unless otherwise stated. When measuring milk we have used the exact conversion of 568 ml (1 pint).
* Size 4 eggs should be used except when otherwise stated.
† Granulated sugar is used unless otherwise stated.

OVEN TEMPERATURE CHART

°C	°F	Gas mark
110	225	$\frac{1}{4}$
130	250	$\frac{1}{2}$
140	275	1
150	300	2
170	325	3
180	350	4
190	375	5
200	400	6
220	425	7
230	450	8
240	475	9

KEY TO SYMBOLS

$\boxed{1.00^*}$ Indicates minimum preparation and cooking times in hours and minutes. They do not include prepared items in the list of ingredients; calculated times apply only to the method. An asterisk * indicates extra time should be allowed, so check the note below symbols.

♨ Chef's hats indicate degree of difficulty of a recipe: no hat means it is straightforward; one hat slightly more complicated; two hats indicates that it is for more advanced cooks.

£ Indicates a recipe which is good value for money; £ £ indicates an expensive recipe. No £ symbol indicates an inexpensive recipe.

✳ Indicates that a recipe will freeze. If there is no symbol, the recipe is unsuitable for freezing. An asterisk * indicates special freezer instructions so check the note immediately below the symbols.

$\boxed{309\ cals}$ Indicates calories per serving, including any suggestions (e.g. cream, to serve) given in the ingredients.

METRIC CONVERSION SCALE

LIQUID				SOLID		
Imperial	Exact conversion	Recommended ml		Imperial	Exact conversion	Recommended g
$\frac{1}{4}$ pint	142 ml	150 ml		1 oz	28.35 g	25 g
$\frac{1}{2}$ pint	284 ml	300 ml		2 oz	56.7 g	50 g
1 pint	568 ml	600 ml		4 oz	113.4 g	100 g
$1\frac{1}{2}$ pints	851 ml	900 ml		8 oz	226.8 g	225 g
$1\frac{3}{4}$ pints	992 ml	1 litre		12 oz	340.2 g	350 g

For quantities of $1\frac{3}{4}$ pints and over, litres and fractions of a litre have been used.

14 oz	397.0 g	400 g
16 oz (1 lb)	453.6 g	450 g

1 kilogram (kg) equals 2.2 lb.

CAKES AND PASTRIES

There's nothing quite like the aroma of baking coming from the kitchen—even the strongest of wills finds it difficult to resist! And there's nothing to compare with the satisfaction and creative pleasure gained from baking and serving a homemade cake. In this book you'll find lots to inspire you. There are cakes and bakes for every taste and occasion. Sweet and simple, fruity and frosted, chocolate and cheesecakes, delicious dinner party desserts and special occasion gâteaux—they're all here for you and your family and friends to enjoy. Even if you're not an experienced cook, this book is for you: every recipe double tested and with its own photograph, clear and concise instructions, plus step-by-step illustrations to help with the method.

If you feel you need to know more about baking than just recipes, turn to the back of the book where you'll find a section simply packed with helpful information to give you confidence. How to choose the right ingredients and equipment, plus tricks of the trade, what to do if anything does go wrong and how to put it right. There is also information on storing and freezing, decorating and the art of piping, plus recipes for making all the different types of cakes, pastries and biscuits.

Everyday Cakes

Don't think of homemade cakes as something to be reserved for special occasions. There are so many delicious everyday cakes using inexpensive store-cupboard ingredients that can be made in next to no time.

Choose a cake from this chapter and give your family and friends a midweek treat.

VICTORIAN SEED CAKE

| 1.30* | £ ✳ | 363 cals |

* plus 1–2 hours cooling

Serves 8

175 g (6 oz) butter

175 g (6 oz) caster sugar

5 ml (1 tsp) vanilla flavouring

3 eggs, beaten

110 g (4 oz) plain flour

110 g (4 oz) self-raising flour

10 ml (2 tsp) caraway seeds

15–30 ml (1–2 tbsp) milk (optional)

1 Grease an 18-cm (7-inch) round cake tin. Line with greaseproof paper and grease the paper.

2 Put the butter, sugar and flavouring into a bowl and beat until pale and fluffy. Beat in the eggs a little at a time.

3 Fold in the flours with the caraway seeds, adding a little milk if necessary to give a dropping consistency.

4 Turn the mixture into the prepared tin. Bake in the oven at 180°C (350°F) mark 4 for about 1 hour until firm to the touch. Turn out on to a wire rack to cool for 1–2 hours.

SEED CAKE

Seed cake is one of the oldest traditional English cakes. It is said to have been made on the farms to celebrate the completion of sowing in the spring and, with caraway seeds much recommended as an aid to digestion, was popular with cottagers and gentry alike.

This Victorian version is lighter than the older farmhouse seed cakes and would have been eaten with tea in many a nursery and elegant drawing room.

MAIDS OF HONOUR

0.45* £ ✳ 143 cals

* plus overnight draining, 1½–2 hours setting, 2–3 hours chilling and 30 minutes cooling

Makes 12

568 ml (1 pint) milk

15 ml (1 tbsp) rennet

212-g (7½-oz) packet frozen puff pastry, thawed, or ¼ quantity puff pastry (see page 148)

1 egg, beaten

15 g (½ oz) butter, melted

50 g (2 oz) caster sugar

1 Warm the milk in a saucepan over a low heat to 37°C (98°F). Remove the pan from the heat and stir in the rennet. Leave for 1½–2 hours until set.

3 Grease twelve 6.5-cm (2½-inch) patty tins. On a lightly floured surface, roll out the pastry very thinly and using a 7.5 cm (3 inch) plain cutter, cut out twelve rounds. Line the patty tins with the pastry rounds and prick well.

4 Stir the egg, melted butter and sugar into the drained, chilled curd. Then divide the mixture between the pastry cases and bake in the oven at 200°C (400°F) mark 6 for 30 minutes until well risen and just firm to the touch. Transfer to a wire rack to cool completely for about 30 minutes.

2 When set, put the junket into a muslin bag and leave to drain overnight. Next day, refrigerate the curd for 2–3 hours or until very firm.

MAIDS OF HONOUR

These are classic little curd tarts said to have been favourites with the maids of honour from Hampton Court in the days of Henry VIII. The recipe was a speciality of a Richmond baker for many years and the tarts are often called 'Richmond' Maids of Honour.

The rennet with which the filling is made is an extract from the stomach lining of a calf, traditionally used to curdle milk for junkets and cheeses. Warm the milk to blood heat before adding the rennet, as the enzyme which sets the milk is more active at this temperature. The junket or 'curds and whey' that form can be eaten alone as a dessert, or drained of the whey to give a simple curd cheese. Curds made like this, then refrigerated until very firm, give a delightfully light, fluffy filling for these miniature cheesecakes.

ALMOND AND CHERRY CAKE

| 1.25* | 🍴 £ £ ✳* | 497 cals |

* plus 1–2 hours chilling; freeze after stage 5

Serves 10

| 275 g (10 oz) glacé cherries |
| 65 g (2½ oz) self-raising flour |
| 225 g (8 oz) unsalted butter, softened |
| 225 g (8 oz) caster sugar |
| 6 eggs, beaten |
| pinch of salt |
| 175 g (6 oz) ground almonds |
| 2.5 ml (½ tsp) almond flavouring |
| icing sugar, to decorate |

1 Grease a deep 23-cm (9-inch) cake tin. Line with greaseproof paper and grease the paper.

2 Dust the cherries lightly with a little of the flour. Arrange in the bottom of the tin.

3 Put the butter and sugar into a bowl and beat together until pale and fluffy. Beat in the eggs a little at a time, adding a little of the flour if the mixture shows signs of curdling.

4 Sift in remaining flour with salt and add the almonds and almond flavouring.

5 Turn the mixture into the prepared tin. Bake in the oven at 180°C (350°F) mark 4 for 1 hour. Cover with greaseproof paper if browning too quickly. Leave in the tin for 1–2 hours to cool. Sift icing sugar on top to decorate.

ALMONDS

The moist fragrance of this delicious Almond and Cherry Cake comes from the ground almonds blended into the mixture. Rich in fat and protein, almonds boost the calorie content of each slice, but they also give an inimitably moist texture.

Ready ground almonds are the easiest to use for this recipe; you can buy them in small 50 g (2 oz) packets or in larger quantities. Beware of buying too many at once as they tend to loose their flavour once the pack is opened. The best flavour comes from nuts that you have ground freshly yourself. Buy them either in the shell or shelled but unblanched. Remove the shells with nut crackers, then soak the kernels in boiling water until the skins will slip off easily. Grind the almonds in a blender or food processor (beware of over-grinding the almonds and turning them to a paste if you use a food processor), or use a nut mill.

FROSTED COCONUT CAKE

| 2.00* | £ | ✳ | 580 cals |

* plus 1 hour cooling

Serves 8

50 g (2 oz) shelled hazel nuts

225 g (8 oz) butter or block
    margarine

225 g (8 oz) caster sugar

5 eggs

2.5 ml ($\frac{1}{2}$ tsp) vanilla flavouring

125 g (4 oz) plain flour

125 g (4 oz) self-raising flour

40 g ($1\frac{1}{2}$ oz) desiccated coconut

75 g (3 oz) icing sugar

shredded coconut

1 Grease a 20-cm (8-inch) base measurement spring-release cake tin. Base-line with grease-proof paper and grease the paper.

2 Spread the nuts out on a baking sheet and brown in the oven at 200°C (400°F) mark 6 for 5–10 minutes. Put into a soft tea towel and rub off the skins. Chop the nuts finely.

3 Put the butter and sugar into a bowl and beat until pale and fluffy. Whisk 4 whole eggs and 1 yolk together and gradually beat into the creamed mixture with the vanilla flavouring.

4 Fold the flours into the mixture with 25 g (1 oz) desiccated coconut, and half the nuts.

5 Turn the mixture into the prepared tin and bake in the oven at 180°C (350°F) mark 4 for 45 minutes.

6 Meanwhile prepare a meringue topping: whisk the egg white until stiff and gradually sift and whisk in the icing sugar, keeping the mixture stiff. Fold in the remaining desiccated coconut and chopped hazel nuts.

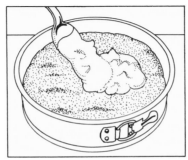

7 Spoon the meringue topping on to the cake, after it has cooked for 45 minutes, and scatter with shredded coconut.

8 Return to the oven for 20–30 minutes or until a skewer comes out of the cake clean. Check after 15 minutes and cover with a layer of greaseproof paper if it is over-browning. Leave to cool completely for 1 hour.

GUERNSEY APPLE CAKE

| 2.00* | £ | ✳ | 337 cals |

* plus 1–2 hours cooling

Serves 8

225 g (8 oz) wholewheat flour

10 ml (2 tsp) freshly ground nutmeg

5 ml (1 tsp) ground cinnamon

10 ml (2 tsp) baking powder

225 g (8 oz) cooking apples, peeled, cored and chopped

125 g (4 oz) butter

225 g (8 oz) soft dark brown sugar

2 eggs, beaten

a little milk (optional)

15 ml (1 tbsp) clear honey

15 ml (1 tbsp) demerara sugar

1 Grease an 18-cm (7-inch) deep round cake tin. Line with greaseproof paper and grease the paper.

2 Add the wholewheat flour, nutmeg, cinnamon and baking powder into a bowl. Mix in the chopped cooking apples.

3 Put the butter and sugar into a bowl and beat until pale and fluffy. Add the eggs, a little at a time, and continue to beat.

4 Fold the flour mixture into the creamed mixture with a little milk, if necessary, to give a dropping consistency.

5 Turn the mixture into the prepared tin. Bake in the oven at 170°C (325°F) mark 3 for about 1½ hours. Turn out on to a wire rack to cool for 1–2 hours. Brush with honey and sprinkle with the demerara sugar to decorate. Eat within 1–2 days.

CINNAMON CHERRY BARS

2.15*	🍴	170 cals

* plus 1 hour cooling

Makes 24

125 g (4 oz) ground almonds

1 egg, beaten

225 g (8 oz) plain flour

225 g (8 oz) caster sugar

175 g (6 oz) soft tub margarine

5 ml (1 tsp) ground cinnamon

grated rind of 1 lemon

125 g (4 oz) black cherry jam

icing sugar, to dredge

1 Lightly grease a 28 × 18 cm (11 × 7 inch) shallow tin. Put the first seven ingredients into a large bowl and beat well.

2 Knead lightly. Cover and refrigerate for at least 30 minutes. Press half the dough evenly into the prepared tin. Spread the jam over the surface.

3 On a lightly floured work surface, lightly knead the remaining dough. With well floured hands, roll into pencil-thin strips. Arrange over the jam to form a close lattice pattern. Refrigerate for 30 minutes.

LAMINGTONS

| 1.30* | ⊟ ⊟ £ ✳* | 340 cals |

* plus 30 minutes cooling and 30 minutes setting; freeze after stage 6

Makes 12

50 g (2 oz) butter

65 g (2½ oz) plain flour

15 ml (1 tbsp) cornflour

3 eggs, size 2

75 g (3 oz) caster sugar

450 g (1 lb) icing sugar

75 g (3 oz) cocoa

100 ml (4 fl oz) milk

75 g (3 oz) desiccated coconut

1 Grease a 28 × 18 cm (11 × 7 inch) cake tin. Line the tin with greaseproof paper and grease the paper.

2 Melt 40 g (1½ oz) butter and let it stand for a few minutes for the salt and any sediment to settle. Sift the flour and cornflour.

3 Put the eggs and sugar into a large bowl and whisk until light and creamy—the mixture should be thick enough to leave a trail on the surface for a few seconds when the whisk is lifted. If whisking by hand, place the bowl over simmering water, then remove from the heat and whisk for 5–10 minutes until cool.

4 Re-sift the flours and fold half into the egg mixture with a metal spoon.

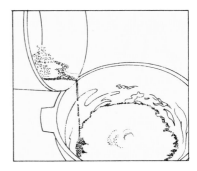

5 Pour the cooled but still flowing butter round the edge of the mixture, taking care not to let the salt and sediment run in.

6 Fold the butter very lightly into the mixture, alternating with the rest of the flour.

7 Turn the mixture into the tin. Bake in the oven at 190°C (375°F) mark 5 until firm to the touch, 20–25 minutes. Turn out on to a wire rack and leave to cool.

8 Meanwhile, for the icing: sift the icing sugar and cocoa into the top part of a double boiler or into a heatproof bowl placed over simmering water.

9 Add the remaining butter and the milk and stir over a gentle heat to a coating consistency.

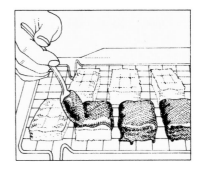

4 Bake at 180°C (350°F) mark 4 for 40 minutes. Cool for 1 hour; dredge with icing sugar. Cut into 24 bars and ease out of the tin. Wrap and store in an airtight tin for up to 1 week.

10 Cut the cake into twelve even-sized pieces. Place on a wire cooling rack. Spoon the icing over each cake to cover. Sprinkle the tops of each with coconut. Leave for 30 minutes until set.

ENGLISH MADELEINES

| 1.20 | 〇 | £ | ✳* | 239 cals |

* freeze after stage 3

Makes 10

100 g (4 oz) butter or block
   margarine

100 g (4 oz) caster sugar

2 eggs, beaten

100 g (4 oz) self-raising flour

30 ml (2 tbsp) red jam, sieved and
   melted

50 g (2 oz) desiccated coconut

5 glacé cherries, halved, and
   angelica pieces, to decorate

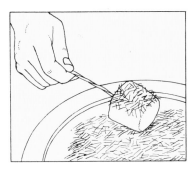

1 Grease ten dariole moulds. Put
the butter and sugar into a
bowl and beat together until pale
and fluffy. Add the eggs a little at
a time, beating well after each
addition. Fold in half the flour,
using a tablespoon. Fold in rest.

2 Turn the mixture into the
moulds, filling them three-
quarters full. Bake in the oven at
180°C (350°F) mark 4 for about 20
minutes until well risen and firm
to the touch. Turn out on to a
wire rack to cool for 20 minutes.

3 When the cakes are almost
cold, trim the bases so they
stand firmly and are about the
same height.

4 Spread the coconut out on a
large plate. Spear each cake on
a skewer, brush with melted jam,
then roll in the coconut to coat.

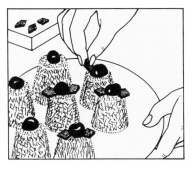

5 Top each madeleine with half
a glacé cherry and small pieces
of angelica.

FRENCH MADELEINES

The continental cousin of the
English madeleine is confusingly
different. Made either from
pastry or a firm, butter-rich cake
mixture such as Genoese sponge,
French madeleines are baked in
shallow, shell-shaped moulds.
They are served undecorated or
lightly dusted with icing sugar.

   French madeleines are a
speciality of the town of
Commercy, in Lorraine. Their
history is said to go back to the
early 18th century and the days
of Stanislas Leszinski, a king of
Poland who became Duke of
Lorraine when ousted from
his homeland.

HALF-POUND CAKE

3.00* £ £ ✳	658 cals

* plus 2 hours cooling

Serves 8

| 225 g (8 oz) butter or margarine |
| 225 g (8 oz) caster sugar |
| 4 eggs, beaten |
| 225 g (8 oz) plain flour |
| 2.5 ml ($\frac{1}{2}$ tsp) salt |
| 2.5 ml ($\frac{1}{2}$ tsp) mixed spice |
| 225 g (8 oz) seedless raisins |
| 225 g (8 oz) mixed currants and sultanas |
| 100 g (4 oz) glacé cherries, halved |
| 15 ml (1 tbsp) brandy |
| a few walnut halves |

1 Grease a 20-cm (8-inch) round cake tin. Line with greaseproof paper and grease the paper.

2 Put the fat and sugar into a bowl and beat together until pale and fluffy. Add the egg a little at a time, beating well after each addition.

3 Sift the flour, salt and spice together into a bowl and stir in the raisins, mixed fruit and cherries. Fold the flour and fruit into the creamed mixture with a metal spoon.

4 Add the brandy and mix to a soft dropping consistency. Turn the mixture into the prepared tin, level the surface and arrange the nuts on top.

5 Bake in the oven at 150°C (300°F) mark 2 for about 2$\frac{1}{2}$ hours. Leave the cake for 15 minutes to cool slightly in the tin, then turn out on to a wire rack to cool completely for 2 hours.

ORANGE-GLAZED GINGER CAKE

| 1.45* | £ | ❋* | 451 cals |

* plus 1 hour setting and 2 hours
cooling; freeze after stage 4

Serves 8

125 g (4 oz) lard

125 g (4 oz) caster sugar

1 egg, beaten

275 g (10 oz) plain flour

7.5 ml (1½ tsp) bicarbonate of
   soda

2.5 ml (½ tsp) salt

5 ml (1 tsp) ground cinnamon

5 ml (1 tsp) ground ginger

100 g (4 oz) golden syrup

100 g (4 oz) black treacle

225 ml (8 fl oz) water

pared rind and juice of 1 orange

1 Grease a 23-cm (9-inch) round
cake tin. Line with greaseproof
paper and grease the paper.

2 Put the lard and sugar into a
bowl and beat together until
pale and fluffy. Beat in the egg,
then the flour, bicarbonate of
soda, salt and spices.

3 Warm together the golden
syrup and black treacle in a
pan with the water and bring to
the boil. Stir into the lard mixture,
beating all the time until completely incorporated.

4 Turn the mixture into the prepared tin. Bake in the oven at
180°C (350°F) mark 4 for about 50
minutes or until a fine warmed
skewer inserted in the centre comes
out clean. Cool in the tin for about
10 minutes before turning out on
to a wire rack to cool completely
for 2 hours.

5 Cut the orange rind into strips;
put into a pan and cover with
water. Boil until tender, about 10
minutes and drain well. Make up
100 g (4 oz) glacé icing (see page
154), using 30 ml (2 tbsp) orange
juice.

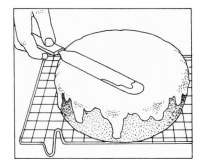

6 Evenly coat the top of the cake
and leave to set for 1 hour.
Sprinkle the orange strips around
the top.

THE GILT ON THE GINGERBREAD

Medieval gingerbread would
have been made with honey, not
treacle or syrup, but it would
have been spiced much the same
as this cake. For sale in the
markets and fairgrounds it was
made in large slabs. Decorative
patterns were traditionally made
on the bread, sometimes with real
gold leaf, and spices such as
cloves, of which the heads might
be gilded. Our strips of orange
rind may seem a poor substitute,
but they go well with the spices.

LEMON SWISS ROLL

1.00*	⊟	£	✳*	376–502 cals

* plus 1 hour setting and 30 minutes cooling; freeze after stage 4

Serves 6–8

3 eggs, size 2

100 g (4 oz) caster sugar

100 g (4 oz) plain flour

150 ml (5 fl oz) double cream

about 275 g (10 oz) lemon curd

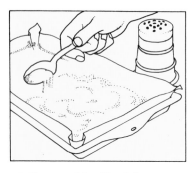

1 Grease a 33 × 23 × 1.5 cm (13 × 9 × ½ inch) Swiss roll tin. Line the base with greaseproof paper and grease the paper. Dust with caster sugar and flour.

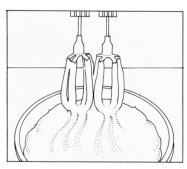

2 Whisk the eggs and sugar in a bowl until thick enough to leave a trail on the surface when the whisk is lifted. Sift in flour and fold gently through the mixture.

3 Turn the mixture into the prepared tin and level the surface. Bake in the oven at 200°C (400°F) mark 6 for 10–12 minutes or until the cake springs back when pressed lightly with a finger and has shrunk away a little from the tin.

4 Sugar a sheet of greaseproof paper and turn the cake out on to it. Roll up with the paper inside. Transfer to a wire rack and leave to cool for 30 minutes.

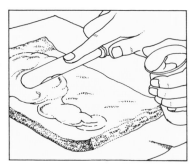

5 Whip the cream until it just holds its shape. Unroll the Swiss roll and spread with three quarters of the lemon curd. Top with cream then roll up again and place on a serving plate.

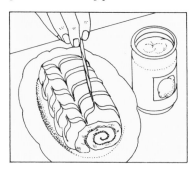

6 Make 100 g (4 oz) glacé icing (see page 154), using 20 ml (4 tsp) water and spoon on to the Swiss roll. Immediately, using the point of a teaspoon, draw rough lines of lemon curd across the icing and pull a skewer through to form a feather pattern. Leave to set, about 1 hour.

SAFFRON CAKE

| 2.30* | ⬜ | £ £ | ✳ | 393 cals |

* plus 2 hours infusing and 1–2 hours cooling

Serves 8

25 g (1 oz) fresh yeast or 7.5 ml
  (1½ tsp) dried yeast plus a pinch
  of sugar

150 ml (¼ pint) tepid milk

450 g (1 lb) strong plain flour

5 ml (1 tsp) salt

50 g (2 oz) butter, cut into pieces

50 g (2 oz) lard, cut into pieces

175 g (6 oz) currants

finely grated rind of ½ a lemon

25 g (1 oz) caster sugar

2.5 ml (½ tsp) saffron strands,
  infused for 2 hours in 150 ml
  (¼ pint) boiling water

1 Grease a 20-cm (8-inch) round cake tin. Crumble the fresh yeast into a bowl and cream with the milk, until smooth. If using the dried yeast and sugar, sprinkle the mixture into the milk and leave in a warm place for 15 minutes until frothy.

2 Sift the flour and salt into a bowl. Rub in the butter and lard until the mixture resembles fine breadcrumbs. Stir in the currants, lemon rind and sugar.

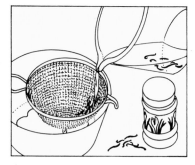

3 Strain the saffron infusion into a pan and warm slightly. Add to the dry ingredients with the yeast liquid and beat well.

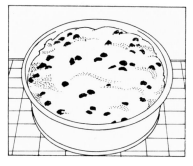

4 Turn the dough into the prepared tin, cover with a clean cloth and leave to rise in a warm place for about 1 hour until the dough comes to the top of the tin.

5 Bake in the oven at 200°C (400°F) mark 6 for 30 minutes. Lower the oven temperature to 180°C (350°F) mark 4 and bake for a further 30 minutes. Turn out on to a wire rack to cool for 1–2 hours.

ALMOND AND HAZEL NUT BARQUETTES

*1.45** £	225 cals

* plus 30 minutes cooling

Makes 8

125 g (4 oz) plain flour

25 g (1 oz) icing sugar plus 60 ml (4 tbsp)

50 g (2 oz) butter, cut into pieces

1 egg, separated

75 g (3 oz) hazel nuts

25 g (1 oz) ground almonds

15 ml (1 tbsp) caster sugar

5 ml (1 tsp) water

1 egg white, for frosting

1 Have ready eight barquettes or boat moulds about 11.5 cm (4½ inches) in length.

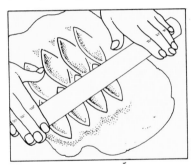

2 Sift together the flour and 25 g (1 oz) icing sugar. Rub in the butter until the mixture resembles fine breadcrumbs. Add the egg yolk and bind to a smooth dough adding a little water, if necessary. Refrigerate for 20 minutes then roll out and use to line the moulds.

3 Spread the hazel nuts out on a baking sheet; brown in oven at 200°C (400°F) mark 6 for 5–10 minutes. Cool, then finely chop, leaving the skins on. Mix with the ground almonds.

4 Lightly beat one egg white with the caster sugar until frothy. Beat in the nut mixture and water.

5 Spoon a little of the mixture into each lined mould. Bake in the oven at 190°C (375°F) mark 5 for 15–20 minutes.

6 For the frosting, sift the remaining icing sugar and beat with just enough egg white to give a coating consistency. Thinly coat each barquette with the icing.

7 Return to the oven for about 5 minutes or until pale golden. Transfer carefully to a wire rack to cool for 30 minutes.

PEANUT CRUNCHIES

1.00* £ ✳	105 cals

*plus 30 minutes cooling

Makes about 24

125 g (4 oz) butter or margarine

125 g (4 oz) soft light brown sugar

45 ml (3 tbsp) peanut butter

225 g (8 oz) plain flour

2.5 ml ($\frac{1}{2}$ tsp) bicarbonate of soda

2.5 ml ($\frac{1}{2}$ tsp) cream of tartar

30 ml (2 tbsp) water

beaten egg, to glaze

50 g (2 oz) salted peanuts

1 Grease a baking sheet. Put the butter into a bowl and beat until creamy. Add the sugar and peanut butter and beat again until pale and fluffy.

2 Sift in flour, bicarbonate of soda and cream of tartar. Using a fork, work dry ingredients in with water to form a soft mixture. Cover; chill for 20 minutes.

3 Turn out on to a lightly floured surface, knead into a ball and roll out fairly thinly. Cut out about 24 biscuits using a 5-cm (2-inch) cutter. Re-knead trimmings as necessary and roll out again.

4 Place on the prepared baking sheet. Brush with beaten egg and press a few peanuts into the centre of each to decorate. Bake in the oven at 190°C (375°F) mark 5 for 20 minutes until crisp and golden. Turn on to a wire rack to cool for 30 minutes.

BROWN SUGAR WHEATMEALS

1.00* £ ✳	98 cals

*plus 30 minutes cooling

Makes about 20

175 g (6 oz) plain wheatmeal flour

1.25 ml ($\frac{1}{4}$ tsp) bicarbonate of soda

1.25 ml ($\frac{1}{4}$ tsp) salt

50 g (2 oz) light soft brown sugar

75 g (3 oz) butter or block margarine, cut into pieces

125 g (4 oz) currants

50 g (2 oz) oatflakes

1 egg, beaten

about 15 ml (1 tbsp) water

1 Grease two baking sheets. Add the flour, bicarbonate of soda, salt and sugar into a bowl. Rub in the fat until the mixture resembles fine breadcrumbs.

2 Stir in the currants and oat-flakes, then stir in the beaten egg and just enough water to bind the mixture together. Knead in the bowl until smooth. Cover and refrigerate for 20 minutes.

3 On a lightly floured surface, roll the dough out to about 5 mm ($\frac{1}{4}$ inch) thickness. Cut into rounds with a 6.5-cm ($2\frac{1}{2}$-inch) fluted cutter and remove centres with a 2.5-cm (1-inch) cutter.

4 Carefully transfer the rings to the prepared baking sheets. Re-roll trimmings as necessary. Refrigerate for at least 20 minutes.

5 Bake in the oven at 190°C (375°F) mark 5 for about 15 minutes until firm. Transfer to a wire rack to cool for 30 minutes.

Left to right:
Honey Jumbles, Peanut crunchies,
Brown Sugar Wheatmeals

Honey Jumbles

| *1.00** | ◻ | £ | 86 cals |

* plus 1½ hours chilling and 30 minutes cooling

Makes 32

150 g (5 oz) soft tub margarine
150 g (5 oz) caster sugar
few drops of vanilla flavouring
finely grated rind of 1 lemon
1 egg, beaten
225 g (8 oz) plain flour
clear honey, to glaze
demerara sugar, to sprinkle

1 Put the margarine and sugar into a bowl and beat until pale and fluffy. Beat in the vanilla flavouring, lemon rind and egg.

2 Stir in the flour, mix to a firm paste. Knead lightly, cover and chill for 30 minutes.

3 Roll the dough into a sausage shape — 5 cm (2 inches) in diameter, 20 cm (8 inches) long. Wrap in greaseproof paper. Chill for 30 minutes.

4 Lightly grease two baking sheets. Cut the chilled dough into 5-mm (¼-inch) rounds. Roll into pencil-thin strips 10 cm (4 inches) long. Twist into 'S' shapes and place on the prepared baking sheets. Refrigerate for 30 minutes.

5 Bake in the oven at 190°C (375°F) mark 5 for 12–15 minutes until pale golden.

6 Remove from the oven and while still warm, brush well with honey, sprinkle with demerara sugar and grill for 1–2 minutes until caramelised.

7 Transfer to a wire rack to cool for 30 minutes. Wrap and store in an airtight tin for up to 3 weeks.

MARZIPAN PINEAPPLE CAKE

1.15* £ £ ✳* 455 cals

* plus 1 hour cooling; freeze after stage 5

Serves 8

175 g (6 oz) butter

150 g (5 oz) soft light brown sugar

finely grated rind of 1 lemon plus 15 ml (1 tbsp) juice

finely grated rind of 1 orange plus 15 ml (1 tbsp) juice

2 eggs, size 2

2 egg yolks

125 g (4 oz) self-raising flour

50 g (2 oz) cornflour

pinch of salt

75 g (3 oz) glacé pineapple, thinly sliced

75 g (3 oz) firm bought marzipan, cut into small cubes

glacé icing (see page 154) using 75 g (3 oz) icing sugar and 15–30 ml (1–2 tbsp) lemon juice instead of water

1 Grease a 24 × 18-cm (9½ × 7-inch) cake or roasting tin. Line with greaseproof paper and grease the paper.

2 Put the butter and sugar into a bowl and beat together until pale and fluffy. Stir in the lemon and orange rind.

3 Lightly beat in the whole eggs and the yolks. Lightly beat in the self-raising flour, cornflour and salt with the orange and lemon juice. Fold in the pineapple.

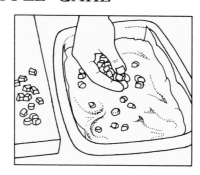

4 Turn the mixture into the prepared tin, level the surface and scatter with marzipan cubes.

5 Bake in the oven at 180°C (350°F) mark 4 for about 45 minutes or until a fine warmed skewer inserted in the centre comes out clean.

6 Meanwhile, make the glacé icing. When the cake is baked, turn it out on to a wire rack and immediately brush the top with the glacé icing. Leave to cool completely for about 1 hour.

GLACÉ FRUITS

Glacé fruits are very expensive to buy because of the labour involved and the amount of sugar used. But they are not difficult to make at home if you have the patience to give them a little attention each day for between 2 and 3 weeks.

The fruit is first lightly cooked and then preserved by a process of slow impregnation with sugar.

If done at home, the preserving takes about 14 days, during which time the fruit is soaked in a heavy syrup, the strength of which is increased daily until the fruit can take up no more. The preserved fruit is then dried in a warm place for several days. The glacé finish is achieved by dipping the preserved fruit in a fresh syrup and drying to a shiny glaze.

Fruit Cakes and Teabreads

Traditional, tried and tested recipes are the ones for teatime—you'll find them all in this chapter. Simple to make, moist and 'moreish' to eat, they keep fresh and fruity right down to the last crumb.

Slice them thickly and serve them plain, or be extravagantly naughty—and spread with butter. They'll taste just as good whichever way you serve them.

DUNDEE CAKE

| 3.00* | 🍽 | ❄ | 434 cals |

* plus 2¼ hours cooling; store for at
least 1 week before eating

Serves 12

| 100 g (4 oz) currants |
| 100 g (4 oz) seedless raisins |
| 50 g (2 oz) blanched almonds, chopped |
| 100 g (4 oz) chopped mixed peel |
| 275 g (10 oz) plain flour |
| 225 g (8 oz) butter or block margarine |
| 225 g (8 oz) soft light brown sugar |
| finely grated rind of 1 lemon |
| 4 eggs, beaten |
| 25 g (1 oz) split almonds, to decorate |

1 Grease a 20-cm (8-inch) round cake tin. Line with greaseproof paper and grease the paper. Combine the fruit, chopped nuts and mixed peel in a bowl. Sift in a little flour and stir until the fruit is evenly coated.

2 Put the butter and sugar into a bowl and beat together until pale and fluffy, then beat in the lemon rind.

3 Add the eggs to the creamed mixture a little at a time, beating well after each addition.

4 Sift the remaining flour over the mixture and fold in lightly with a metal spoon, then fold in the fruit and nut mixture.

5 Turn the mixture into the prepared tin and make a slight hollow in the centre with the back of a metal spoon. Arrange the split almonds on the top.

6 Bake in the oven at 170°C (325°F) mark 3 for about 2½ hours until a fine warmed skewer inserted in the centre comes out clean. Check near the end of the cooking time and cover with several layers of greaseproof paper if it is overbrowning.

7 Cool in the tin for 15 minutes, before turning out on to a wire rack to cool completely for 2 hours. Store in an airtight tin for at least 1 week to mature.

DRIED FRUIT

Currants, raisins and sultanas are all dried grapes of different varieties. Currants are small black seedless grapes originating in the Corinth region of Greece (hence the name); they are also produced in other countries, especially Australia. Seedless raisins are slightly larger than currants, produced mainly in Spain, Australia and the United States. Dessert raisins are the large Muscatel grape and have to be stoned before cooking but the flavour is excellent. Sultanas are small white seedless grapes grown in Turkey, Australia and the United States.

When choosing dried fruit for a cake, look for plump, juicy fruits. Good brands are sold ready washed but look them over carefully. Unwashed fruits are cheaper, but must be washed well, drained and left to dry spread out over muslin; let them dry thoroughly, but don't place them over direct heat because this tends to make them hard. Should dried fruit become hard from long storage, soak in hot water, then drain and dry off.

CHERRY AND COCONUT CAKE

2.00*	✳	336–420 cals

*plus 1 hour cooling

Serves 8–10

250 g (9 oz) self-raising flour

1.25 ml ($\frac{1}{4}$ tsp) salt

125 g (4 oz) butter or block
   margarine, cut into pieces

75 g (3 oz) desiccated coconut

125 g (4 oz) caster sugar

125 g (4 oz) glacé cherries, finely
   chopped

2 eggs, size 6, beaten

225 ml (8 fl oz) milk

25 g (1 oz) shredded coconut

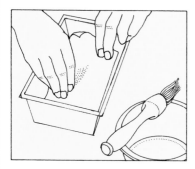

1 Grease a 1.3-litre (2$\frac{1}{4}$-pint)
loaf tin. Base-line with greaseproof paper, grease the paper and
dust with flour.

2 Put the flour and salt into a
bowl and rub in the fat until
the mixture resembles fine breadcrumbs. Stir in the coconut, sugar
and cherries.

3 Whisk together the eggs and
milk and beat into the dry ingredients. Turn the mixture into
the tin, level the surface and scatter
over the shredded coconut.

4 Bake in the oven at 180°C
(350°F) mark 4 for 1$\frac{1}{2}$ hours
until a fine warmed skewer inserted in the centre comes out
clean. Check after 40 minutes and
cover with greaseproof paper if
overbrowning. Turn out on to a
wire rack to cool for 1 hour.

FRUIT CRUSTED CIDER CAKE

1.15*	🍴	£	268–334 cals

* plus 1 hour cooling

Serves 8–10

45 ml (3 tbsp) golden syrup
150 g (5 oz) butter or block margarine
350 g (12 oz) cooking apples, peeled, cored and finely chopped
45 ml (3 tbsp) mincemeat
50 g (2 oz) cornflakes, crushed
125 g (4 oz) caster sugar
2 eggs, beaten
125 g (4 oz) self-raising flour
45 ml (3 tbsp) dry cider

1 Line a 35.5 × 11.5 cm (14 × 4½ inch) shallow rectangular tart frame with foil. Grease the foil. Put the syrup into a pan with 25 g (1 oz) butter and melt. Add apples, mincemeat, cornflakes. Set aside.

2 Put the remaining butter and the sugar into a bowl and beat together until pale and fluffy. Gradually beat in the eggs.

3 Fold the flour into the mixture. Pour in the cider and mix it in. Turn the mixture into the prepared frame and level the surface. Spread the apple mixture evenly over it.

4 Bake in the oven at 170°C (325°F) mark 3 for 45–50 minutes or until firm to the touch. Cool in the metal frame for 1 hour, then cut into bars for serving.

GINGERBREAD SLAB

1.40* £ ✳ 121–145 cals

* plus 1 hour cooling; store for at least
2 days before eating

Makes 20–24 slices

125 g (4 oz) black treacle

125 g (4 oz) golden syrup

50 g (2 oz) butter or block
 margarine

50 g (2 oz) lard

225 g (8 oz) plain flour

1.25 ml ($\frac{1}{4}$ tsp) bicarbonate of soda

5 ml (1 tsp) mixed spice

5 ml (1 tsp) ground ginger

100 g (4 oz) dark soft brown sugar

150 ml ($\frac{1}{4}$ pint) milk

1 Grease an 18-cm (7-inch)
square cake tin. Base-line with
greaseproof paper and then grease
the paper.

2 Put the black treacle, golden
syrup, butter or margarine and
lard into a saucepan and heat
gently to melt the mixture.

3 Sift the flour, bicarbonate of
soda and spices into a bowl
and stir in the sugar.

4 Make a well in the centre of
the dry ingredients and pour
in the milk and the treacle mixture.
Beat well until smooth and of a
thick pouring consistency.

5 Turn into the prepared tin and
bake in the oven at 170°C
(325°F) mark 3 for 1–1$\frac{1}{4}$ hours or
until a fine warmed skewer in-
serted in the centre of the cake
comes out clean.

6 Cool in the tin for 1 hour.
Remove from tin, wrap and
store for at least 2 days in an
airtight tin before eating. Serve
sliced, plain or buttered.

DATE AND ORANGE BARREL TEABREAD

1.30*	£	✳	175–219 cals

*plus 1 hour cooling

Serves 8–10

200 g (7 oz) plain flour

5 ml (1 tsp) baking powder

5 ml (1 tsp) bicarbonate of soda

65 g (2½ oz) butter or block margarine, cut into pieces

65 g (2½ oz) soft light brown sugar

75 g (3 oz) stoned dates, snipped

finely grated rind of 1 orange plus 45 ml (3 tbsp) of the juice

about 90 ml (6 tbsp) milk

½ quantity orange buttercream (see page 154) and a piece of candied orange peel, to decorate

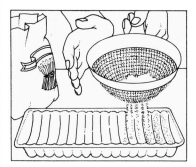

1 Grease and flour a 25.5-cm (10-inch) Balmoral tin or a 900-ml (1½-pint) loaf tin.

2 Sift the flour, baking powder and bicarbonate of soda into a bowl. Rub in the butter until the mixture resembles fine bread-crumbs. Stir in the sugar and mix well until evenly incorporated.

3 Stir in the dates and the orange rind. Add the orange juice and enough milk to make a soft dough.

4 Carefully turn the mixture into the prepared tin. Stand it on a baking sheet, grease another baking sheet and place it, greased side down, on top of the tin.

5 Bake in the oven at 180°C (350°F) mark 4 for 1 hour or until a fine warmed skewer inserted in the centre comes out clean and dry.

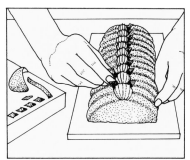

6 Turn out on to a wire rack to cool for 1 hour. Wrap and store for 1 day in an airtight tin before eating. To serve, make the buttercream and pipe along the top of the cake. Decorate with small diamonds of cut orange peel.

CRUSTLESS CAKES

You may think this is a strange way to bake a cake, covered with a baking sheet, but it achieves a special effect. Being totally sur-rounded by tin, the cake forms no crust and the inside stays par-ticularly moist. Professional bakers have special tins with lids to achieve the same effect (think of the square 'sandwich' loaf that has no risen, crisp crust). With a stiff yeast dough the loaf can be baked *under* the tin. This mix-ture is too moist for that method, it would simply run out of the tin, so placing a sheet on top is the easy way out. A fluted Bal-moral tin gives the full 'barrel' effect, but a loaf tin can be used instead of a Balmoral tin.

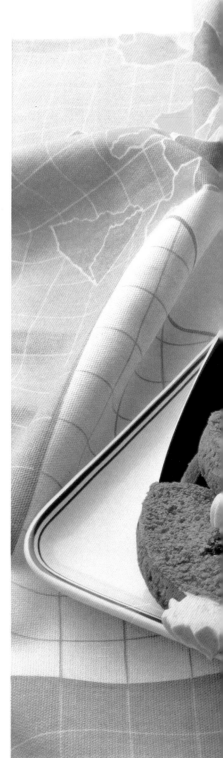

PRUNE AND NUT TEABREAD

| 1.30* | ☐ | ✳ | 261–326 cals |

* plus 1 hour cooling; wrap and store for 1–2 days before slicing

Serves 8–10

275 g (10 oz) self-raising flour

pinch of salt

7.5 ml (1½ tsp) ground cinnamon

75 g (3 oz) butter or block margarine, cut into pieces

75 g (3 oz) demerara sugar

1 egg, beaten

100 ml (4 fl oz) milk

50 g (2 oz) shelled walnuts, chopped

100 g (4 oz) pitted tenderised prunes

15 ml (1 tbsp) clear honey

1 Grease a 2-litre (3½-pint) loaf tin. Base-line the loaf tin with greaseproof paper and grease the paper.

2 Sift the flour and salt into a bowl and add the cinnamon. Rub in the fat until the mixture resembles fine breadcrumbs.

3 Stir in the sugar, and make a well in the centre. Add the egg and milk and gradually draw in the dry ingredients to form a smooth dough.

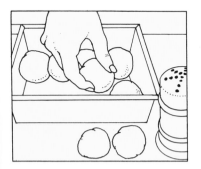

4 Using floured hands shape the mixture into sixteen even-sized rounds. Place eight in the base of the tin. Sprinkle over half the nuts.

5 Snip the prunes and sprinkle on top of the nuts. Place the remaining dough rounds on top and sprinkle over the remaining chopped walnuts.

6 Bake in the oven at 190°C (375°F) mark 5 for about 50 minutes or until firm to the touch. Check near the end of cooking time and cover with greaseproof paper if it is overbrowning.

7 Turn out on to a wire rack to cool for 1 hour. When cold brush with the honey to glaze. Wrap and store for 1–2 days in an airtight tin before slicing and buttering.

TEABREADS

A teabread mixture is usually less rich than cake, but no less delicious for that. Serve it sliced and thickly buttered, like good fresh bread. It is excellent served with afternoon tea or mid-morning coffee, or try it occasionally as a lunchtime pudding. A fruity teabread like this one improves as it matures, the flavour and moisture from the fruit penetrating the cake and mellowing it over a number of days.

In continental Europe it is traditional to serve sweet breads for breakfast, with either butter or cheese. Try thin slices of Edam or Gouda cheese, or spread with curd cheese instead of butter and omit the cheese.

GINGER MARMALADE TEABREAD

| 1.30* | £ | ✳ | 167–208 cals |

* plus 1 hour cooling

Serves 8–10

200 g (7 oz) plain flour

5 ml (1 tsp) ground ginger

5 ml (1 tsp) baking powder

40 g (1½ oz) block margarine

65 g (2½ oz) soft light brown sugar

60 ml (4 tbsp) ginger marmalade

1 egg, beaten

60 ml (4 tbsp) milk

40 g (1½ oz) stem ginger, chopped

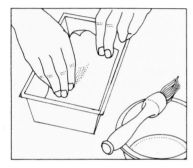

1 Grease a 900-ml (1½-pint) loaf tin with melted lard. Base-line with greaseproof paper and grease the paper.

2 Put the flour, ginger and baking powder into a bowl and rub in fat until mixture resembles fine breadcrumbs. Stir in sugar.

3 Mix together the marmalade, egg and most of the milk. Stir into the dry ingredients and add the rest of the milk, if necessary, to mix to a soft dough.

4 Turn the mixture into the prepared tin, level the surface and press pieces of ginger on top. Bake in the oven at 170°C (325°F) mark 3 for about 1 hour or until golden. Turn out on to a wire rack for 1 hour to cool.

ECCLES CAKES

| 1.00* | 🍴 | ✳ | 167–209 cals |

* plus 30 minutes cooling

Makes 8–10

212-g (7½-oz) packet frozen puff
  pastry, thawed, or ¼ quantity
  puff or flaky pastry (see page
  148 and 149)

25 g (1 oz) butter, softened

25 g (1 oz) soft dark brown sugar

25 g (1 oz) finely chopped mixed
  peel

50 g (2 oz) currants

caster sugar

1 Roll out the pastry on a lightly
floured working surface and
cut into eight to ten 9-cm (3½-
inch) rounds.

2 For the filling: mix the butter,
sugar, mixed peel and currants
in a bowl.

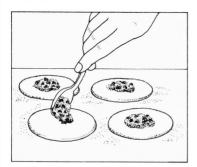

3 Place 5 ml (1 tsp) of the fruit
and butter mixture in the
centre of each pastry round. Draw
up the edges of each pastry round
to enclose the filling and then re-
shape.

4 Turn each round over and roll
lightly until the currants just
show through.

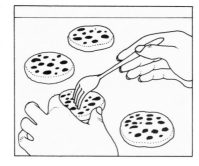

5 Prick the top of each with a
fork. Allow the pastry rounds
to 'rest' for about 10 minutes in a
cool place.

6 Dampen a baking sheet and
transfer the rounds to it. Bake
in the oven at 230°C (450°F)
mark 8 for about 15 minutes until
golden. Transfer to a wire rack to
cool for 30 minutes. Sprinkle with
caster sugar while still warm.

ECCLES CAKES

Dripping with butter and loaded
with currants, Eccles cakes are
among the nation's favourite re-
gional pastries. It is not just in
Lancashire that village bakeries
are obliged to produce them in
large quantities every morning.
Some versions are made with
shortcrust pastry, others favour
the richer puff or flaky pastries
suggested here, either way the
pastry must be rolled really
thinly, so that the dark fruit
shows through. Take care that it
does not burst though.

Eccles cakes are at their best
very fresh, preferably still slightly
warm from the oven. If you want
to make them for eating next day
do not sprinkle with caster sugar;
store them in an airtight tin when
cold then reheat the next day and
sprinkle with sugar after they
come out of the oven.

TRADITIONAL CAKE-IN-THE-PAN

| 0.35 | £ | ✳ | 437 cals |

Serves 4

225 g (8 oz) wholewheat self-raising flour

pinch of salt

pinch of freshly grated nutmeg

50 g (2 oz) lard, cut into pieces

50 g (2 oz) caster sugar

100 g (4 oz) seedless raisins

150 ml ($\frac{1}{4}$ pint) water

1 Sift the flour, salt and nutmeg together into a bowl. Rub in the lard, add the caster sugar and seedless raisins.

2 Mix with the cold water to make a soft dough and divide into four.

3 Form each quarter of dough into a ball and roll out into a round about 12.5 cm (5 inches) in diameter.

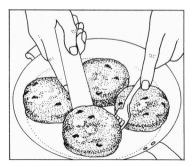

4 Lightly grease a frying pan and place over low heat. Cook the rounds for about 10 minutes on each side. Serve at once.

HONEY HAZEL NUT TWIST

3.00* 🄯 ✳ 139–166 cals

* plus 1 hour cooling
Serves 10–12

60 ml (4 tbsp) tepid milk
15 ml (1 tbsp) caster sugar
5 ml (1 tsp) dried yeast
175 g (6 oz) strong plain flour
2.5 ml (½ tsp) salt
75 g (3 oz) butter or block margarine, cut into pieces
1 egg, size 6
50 g (2 oz) shelled hazel nuts
75 ml (5 tbsp) thick honey

1 Lightly oil a bowl and set aside. Grease an 18-cm (7-inch) straight-sided sandwich tin. Base-line with greaseproof paper and grease the paper.

2 Put the milk into a small bowl and sprinkle over 5 ml (1 tsp) sugar and the yeast. Leave in a warm place for about 15 minutes until frothy.

3 Sift the flour with the salt into a bowl and rub in 50 g (2 oz) of the butter until the mixture resembles fine breadcrumbs. Stir in the remaining sugar and beat in the egg and the yeast liquid to form a soft dough.

4 Turn out on to a lightly floured surface and knead until smooth, about 5 minutes. Put into the oiled bowl, cover with oiled cling film and leave to double in size, about 45 minutes.

5 Meanwhile, spread the nuts out on a baking sheet and brown in the oven at 200°C (400°F) mark 6 for 5–10 minutes. Put into a soft tea towel and rub off the skins. Grind the nuts in an electric blender or food processor.

6 Beat the remaining butter with the nuts and 45 ml (3 tbsp) honey to a smooth paste.

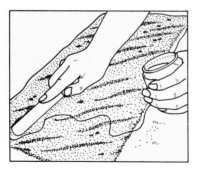

7 Turn the dough out on to a floured surface, knead again lightly and roll out to an oblong 61 × 20 cm (24 × 8 inch). Spread the honey over the surface.

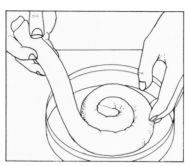

8 Roll up from a long edge. Coil into the prepared sandwich tin. Press down firmly. Cover as in stage 4 and leave to double in size, about 45 minutes.

9 Bake at 200°C (400°F) mark 6 for 20–25 minutes until golden brown. Turn out on to a plate and brush at once with the remaining honey, warmed. Cool for 1 hour before serving.

Chocolate Cakes

Rich and dark, sumptuous and squidgy, the chocolate cakes in this chapter are wickedly good. For morning coffee, afternoon tea or a spectacular dinner party dessert, there are chocolate cakes for every occasion. So go ahead and spoil yourself—you won't be disappointed, whichever one you choose.

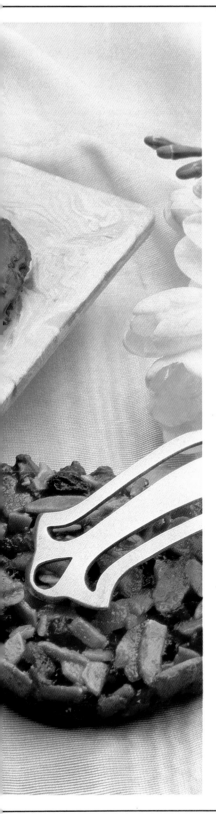

FLORENTINES

| 1.00* | 🎩 | 246 cals |

* plus 1 hour cooling and setting

Makes about 12

90 g (3½ oz) butter

100 g (4 oz) caster sugar

100 g (4 oz) flaked almonds, roughly chopped

25 g (1 oz) sultanas

5 glacé cherries, chopped

25 g (1 oz) chopped mixed peel

15 ml (1 tbsp) single cream or top of the milk

175 g (6 oz) plain chocolate

1 Line three baking sheets with non-stick paper. Melt the butter in a saucepan over a low heat, add the sugar and boil the mixture for 1 minute.

2 Remove the pan from the heat and add all the remaining ingredients, except the chocolate, stirring well to mix.

3 Drop the mixture in small, well-rounded heaps on to the prepared sheets, allowing enough room between each for the mixture to spread.

4 Bake the biscuit rounds in the oven at 180°C (350°F) mark 4 for 10 minutes until golden brown.

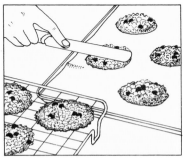

5 Remove from the oven and press around the edges of the biscuits with the blade of a knife to neaten the shape. Leave on the baking sheets for 5 minutes until beginning to firm, then lift on to a wire rack to cool for 20 minutes.

6 Break the chocolate into a heat-proof bowl and place over simmering water. Stir until the chocolate is melted, then remove from the heat and leave to cool for 10–15 minutes.

7 Just as the chocolate is beginning to set, spread it over the backs of the biscuits.

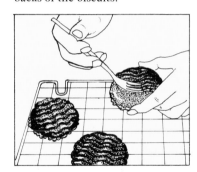

8 Draw the prongs of a fork across the chocolate to mark wavy lines and leave to set for about 30 minutes.

MELTING CHOCOLATE

If chocolate is overheated, it may curdle or thicken instead of melting smoothly. To guard against this, either melt it in a bowl placed over a pan of hot water, as suggested here, or use a double saucepan. If the chocolate does curdle, add a little blended white vegetable fat. Break the fat into small pieces and stir into the chocolate until it reaches the desired consistency.

DEVIL'S FOOD CAKE

2.00* ⬜ ✳* 696 cals

* plus 30 minutes cooling and 1 hour
standing time; freeze after stage 8

Serves 8

75 g (3 oz) plain chocolate plus 25 g (1 oz) (optional)
250 g (9 oz) soft light brown sugar
200 ml (⅓ pint) milk
75 g (3 oz) butter or block margarine
2 eggs
175 g (6 oz) plain flour
3.75 ml (¾ tsp) bicarbonate of soda
450 g (1 lb) caster sugar
120 ml (8 tbsp) water
2 egg whites

1 Lightly brush two 19-cm (7½-inch) sandwich tins with melted lard. Base-line with grease-proof paper and grease the paper. Leave for 5 minutes to set, then dust with sugar and flour.

2 Break 75 g (3 oz) of the chocolate in small pieces into a saucepan. Add 75 g (3 oz) of the brown sugar and the milk. Heat very gently, stirring to dissolve the sugar and blend the ingredients, then remove from the heat and leave to cool for 10 minutes.

3 Put the butter into a bowl and beat until pale and soft. Gradually add the remaining brown sugar and beat until pale and fluffy.

4 Lightly whisk the eggs and gradually beat into the creamed mixture. Slowly add the cooled chocolate mixture beating until combined.

5 Sift the flour and bicarbonate of soda into the creamed mixture and gently fold in using a metal spoon. Turn the mixture into prepared tins, then tap gently to level it.

6 Bake in the oven at 180°C (350°F) mark 4 for about 35 minutes. The cakes are cooked when they spring back when pressed lightly with a finger and have shrunk away a little from the sandwich tins.

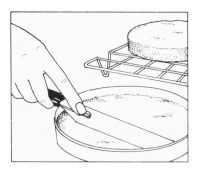

7 Cool in the tins for a couple of minutes before turning out on to a wire rack to cool completely. Ease them away from the tins using a palette knife, taking care not to break the crust.

8 Tap the tins on the work surface to loosen the cakes. Gently pull off the paper and leave to cool.

9 Put the sugar for the frosting in a pan with the water, dissolve over a low heat, then boil rapidly to 115°C (240°F) on a sugar thermometer, or until the mixture reaches the soft ball stage. Check by plunging a teaspoonful into a bowl of iced water. It should form a ball in your fingers.

10 Meanwhile, whisk the egg whites in a large bowl until stiff. Allow the bubbles in the syrup to settle, then slowly pour the hot syrup on to the egg whites, beating constantly. Once all the sugar syrup is added, continue beating until the mixture stands in peaks and just starts to become matt round the edges. (The icing sets quickly, so work rapidly.)

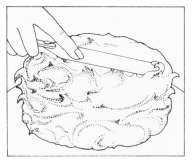

11 Sandwich the cakes together with a little of the frosting. Spread the remaining frosting over the cake with a palette knife. Pull the icing up into peaks all over, then leave the cake for about 30 minutes, to allow the icing to set slightly.

12 Break up the chocolate, if using, and put it in a small bowl over a pan of hot water. Heat gently, stirring, until the chocolate has melted. Dribble the chocolate over the top of the cake with a teaspoon to make a swirl pattern. Leave for 30 minutes before serving.

AMERICAN CAKES

Two classic cakes from America are Angel Food Cake and Devil's Food Cake. The first is an airy vanilla-flavoured sponge. It is very white in colour and light in texture because it is made with flour and egg whites, with no egg yolks. Its opposite number is the rich, moist chocolate cake recipe given here. Generously filled and coated with frosting, Devil's Food Cake is a favourite for serving as a dinnertime dessert, or at coffee parties.

CHOCOLATE COFFEE REFRIGERATOR SLICE

1.00* □ £ £ ✳*

752–1129 cals

* plus 3–4 hours chilling; freeze after stage 7

Serves 4–6

30 ml (2 tbsp) instant coffee granules

250 ml (7 fl oz) boiling water

45 ml (3 tbsp) brandy

125 g (4 oz) plain chocolate

125 g (4 oz) unsalted butter, softened

50 g (2 oz) icing sugar

2 egg yolks

300 ml (10 fl oz) whipping cream

50 g (2 oz) chopped almonds, toasted

about 30 sponge fingers

coffee beans, to decorate

1 Grease a 22 × 11.5 cm (8½ × 4½ inch) top measurement loaf tin and base-line with greaseproof paper. Grease the paper.

2 Make up the coffee granules with the boiling water and stir in the brandy. Set aside to cool for 15 minutes.

3 Break the chocolate into a small heatproof bowl with 15 ml (1 tbsp) water and place over simmering water. Stir until the chocolate is melted then remove from the heat and allow to cool for about 5 minutes.

4 Sift the icing sugar into a bowl. Add the butter and beat them together until pale and fluffy. Add the egg yolks, beating well.

5 Lightly whip the cream and refrigerate half of it. Stir the remaining cream, the cooled chocolate and the nuts into the butter and egg yolk mixture.

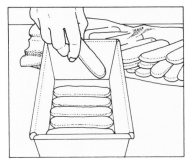

6 Line the bottom of the prepared loaf tin with sponge fingers, cutting to fit if necessary. Spoon over one third of the coffee and brandy mixture.

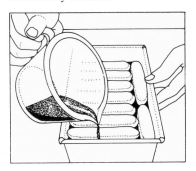

7 Continue layering the chocolate mixture and sponge fingers into the tin, soaking each layer with coffee and ending with soaked sponge fingers. Weight down lightly and refrigerate for 3–4 hours until set.

8 Turn out, remove the paper and decorate with the reserved whipped cream and the coffee beans.

CHOCOLATE AND HAZEL NUT GATEAU

2.00* ⬜ £ ❄* 662 cals

* plus 45 minutes cooling; freeze after stage 2

Serves 10

275 g (10 oz) unsalted butter, softened

225 g (8 oz) soft light brown sugar

4 eggs, separated

100 g (4 oz) self-raising flour

pinch of salt

100 g (4 oz) ground hazel nuts

100 g (4 oz) plain chocolate, finely grated

225 g (8 oz) icing sugar

50 g (2 oz) cocoa powder

30 ml (2 tbsp) milk

25 g (1 oz) chopped hazel nuts, to decorate

1 Grease and line a 23-cm (9-inch) round cake tin. Put 225 g (8 oz) of the butter and the sugar into a bowl and beat together until pale and fluffy. Beat in the egg yolks one at a time, then fold in the flour and salt. Stir in the hazel nuts and chocolate.

2 Whisk the egg whites until stiff, then fold into the cake mixture. Pour into the prepared tin and bake in the oven at 170°C (325°F) mark 3 for 75 minutes or until a fine warmed skewer inserted in the centre comes out clean. Leave to cool in the tin for 45 minutes.

3 Make the fudge icing. Sift the icing sugar and cocoa powder together, then put into a heavy-based pan with the remaining butter and the milk. Heat gently until the butter has melted; beat until smooth. Remove from heat.

4 Cut the cake in half horizontally. Spread a little icing over one half, then top with the other. Swirl remaining icing over and sprinkle with nuts.

RICH CHOCOLATE CAKE

Illustrated on front cover

| 1.30* | ✳ | 858–1144 cals |

* plus 1 hour cooling

Serves 8–10

275 g (10 oz) plain flour

45 ml (3 tbsp) cocoa powder

6.25 ml (1¼ tsp) baking powder

2.5 ml (½ tsp) bicarbonate of soda

large pinch of salt

115 g (4½ oz) plain chocolate

225 g (8 oz) butter

215 g (7½ oz) soft light brown sugar

2 eggs, size 2, beaten

142 g (5 oz) natural yogurt

2.5 ml (½ tsp) vanilla flavouring

175 g (6 oz) icing sugar

15 ml (1 tbsp) milk or warm water

300 ml (10 fl oz) double cream, to
    decorate

chocolate curls, to decorate (see
    page 153)

1 Grease three 18-cm (7-inch)
sandwich tins. Line with
greaseproof paper and grease the
paper.

2 Sift together the flour, cocoa
powder, baking powder, bicarbonate of soda and salt.

3 Break 50 g (2 oz) of the chocolate into a bowl. Place over a
saucepan of simmering water and
heat gently, stirring, until the
chocolate has melted. Leave to
cool for 30 minutes.

4 Cream 150 g (5 oz) of the
butter and the brown sugar
together until light and fluffy.
Beat in the eggs, then fold in the
chocolate, the sifted ingredients,
the yogurt and vanilla flavouring.

5 Turn the mixture into the prepared tins and level the surface.
Bake in the oven at 190°C (375°F)
mark 5 for 25 minutes until risen
and firm to the touch. Turn out
and leave to cool on a wire rack.

6 Meanwhile make the buttercream. Break up the remaining
chocolate in a bowl. Place over a
saucepan of hot water and heat
gently, stirring, until the chocolate
has melted. Leave to cool for 30
minutes.

7 Cream the remaining 75 g
(3 oz) butter until soft and
gradually sift and beat in the icing
sugar, adding the cooled melted
chocolate and the milk or warm
water. Use this buttercream to
sandwich the three cakes together.

8 Whip the double cream until
just stiff and spread a third
evenly over the top of the cake.
Use the rest of the cream to pipe
rosettes around the edge. Finally
fill the centre of the cake with
chocolate curls.

CHOCOLATE FOR COOKING

True cooking chocolate (often
known by the trade name Menier)
is unsweetened and has no extra
fat added; but it is difficult to
obtain. The recipes in this book
have been tested with dessert
chocolate, so if you do use cooking chocolate extra sugar will be
needed.

Always choose plain chocolate
for cooking as milk chocolate
contains condensed or powdered
milk that separates out on heat-
ing (though you can grate it for
decorating if you wish). The
words bitter or semi-sweet on
the label of plain chocolate indicate the amount of sugar added
to the chocolate—either are suitable for cooking.

Chocolate cake coverings and
chocolate sold broken in chunks,
often in a bag without a label,
contain added fats or oils that
make them easy to work with,
but the flavour is not so good.

CHOCOLATE CHEQUERBOARDS

| 2.00 | 🛢 | f | 92 cals |

Makes 32

200 g (7 oz) soft tub margarine
90 g (3½ oz) caster sugar
290 g (10½ oz) plain flour
15 ml (1 tbsp) cocoa powder
vanilla flavouring
beaten white egg

1 Beat together the margarine, sugar and flour to give a workable dough.

2 Remove two-thirds of the dough to another bowl. Into this, work the cocoa powder mixed to a paste with 15 ml (1 tbsp) water. Knead to an even coloured ball. Halve.

3 Work a few drops of vanilla into the remaining plain dough. On a floured surface, roll the vanilla dough into six 1 × 15 cm (½ × 6 inch) strips. Repeat with one piece of the chocolate dough.

4 Assemble the strips into 2 logs. Lay 3 strips, alternating vanilla and chocolate, side by side. Place another 3 strips on top to make a chequerboard pattern. Brush with a little beaten egg.

5 Halve the remaining chocolate dough. Roll out each piece into a sheet large enough to encase a log. Roll round each log and brush with beaten egg white.

6 Straighten up the logs and chill for about 1 hour until very firm. Cut each log into 1-cm (½-inch) slices. Place on lightly greased baking sheets and bake in the oven at 190°C (375°F) mark 5 for about 15–20 minutes. Turn out and cool on a wire rack for 30 minutes. Store in an airtight container for 2–3 weeks.

CHOCOLATE NUT SNAPS

| 1.20* | £ | ✳ | 109 cals |

* plus 1 hour cooling and setting;
freeze after stage 5

Makes 24

| 1 egg, separated |
| 100 g (4 oz) caster sugar |
| 125 g (5 oz) plain chocolate |
| 125 g (4 oz) hazel nuts, finely chopped |
| 40 g (1½ oz) plain flour |
| 200 g (7 oz) icing sugar |
| about 30 ml (2 tbsp) water |

1 Grease two baking sheets.
Whisk the egg white until stiff.
Fold in the caster sugar.

2 Coarsely grate 75 g (3 oz) plain
chocolate into the mixture and
stir in with the hazel nuts, flour
and egg yolk.

3 Turn out on a well floured
surface and knead lightly.
Cover and refrigerate for about
30 minutes.

4 Roll the dough out to 5 mm
(¾ inch) thickness. Using a
5-cm (2-inch) plain cutter, cut out
24 shapes. Knead lightly and place
on the prepared baking sheets.
Cover and refrigerate the biscuits
again for 30 minutes.

5 Bake in the oven at 190°C
(375°F) mark 5 for about 20
minutes until crisp. Immediately
ease off the baking sheet on to a
wire rack to cool for 30 minutes.

6 Break the remaining chocolate
into a heatproof bowl and
place over simmering water. Stir
until the chocolate is melted, then
remove from heat.

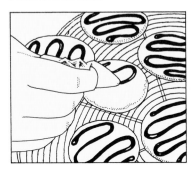

7 Cut the tip off a paper icing
bag and spoon in the melted
chocolate. Pipe lines of chocolate
across the biscuits. Leave to set for
30 minutes. The biscuits can be
stored, un-iced, in airtight containers for 2–3 weeks.

ROLLED BISCUITS

Short biscuit doughs are often
difficult to roll without breaking.
Chilling helps, but you could also
try rolling the dough between
sheets of cling film. This not
only holds the dough together,
but eliminates the need for extra
flour on the board, which can
harden the surface of the baked
biscuits.

After rolling, remove the top
sheet of film to cut the biscuits,
then lift each one on the bottom
piece of cling film to transfer it
to the baking sheet.

BLACK FOREST GÂTEAU

1.45* ☐ £ £ ✱*

516–645 cals

* plus 30 minutes cooling; freeze after stage 5 after cooling

Serves 8–10

100 g (4 oz) butter

6 eggs

225 g (8 oz) caster sugar

75 g (3 oz) plain flour

50 g (2 oz) cocoa powder

2.5 ml ($\frac{1}{2}$ tsp) vanilla flavouring

two 425-g (15-oz) cans stoned black cherries

60 ml (4 tbsp) kirsch

600 ml (20 fl oz) whipping cream

100 g (4 oz) chocolate curls, to decorate (see page 153)

5 ml (1 tsp) arrowroot

1 Grease a 23-cm (9-inch) round cake tin. Line with greaseproof paper and grease the paper. Put the butter into a bowl, stand this over a pan of warm water and beat it until really soft but not melted.

2 Put the eggs and sugar into a large bowl and whisk until thick enough to leave a trail on the surface when the whisk is lifted.

3 Sift the flour and cocoa into the mixture and lightly fold in with a metal spoon. Fold in vanilla flavouring and softened butter.

4 Turn the mixture into the prepared tin, tilt the tin to spread the mixture evenly, and bake in the oven at 180°C (350°F) mark 4 for about 40 minutes until risen and firm to the touch.

5 Turn out of the tin on to a wire rack, covered with greaseproof paper, to cool for 30 minutes. Strain the syrup from the cans of cherries, reserving the cherries, 45 ml (3 tbsp) syrup for the glaze and 75 ml (5 tbsp) syrup for the filling. Add the kirsch to latter syrup.

6 Cut the cake into three horizontally. Place a layer on a flat plate and spoon over 45 ml (3 tbsp) of the kirsch-flavoured syrup.

7 Whip the cream until it holds its shape and spread a little thinly over the soaked sponge. Reserve a quarter of the cherries for decoration and scatter half the remainder over the cream.

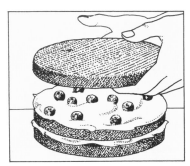

8 Repeat the layers of sponge, syrup, cream and cherries. Top with the third cake round and spoon over the remaining kirsch-flavoured syrup.

9 Spread a thin layer of cream around the sides of the cake, reserving a third to decorate. Press on the chocolate curls, reserving a few to decorate the top.

10 Fill a piping bag, fitted with a large star nozzle, with the remaining whipped cream and pipe whirls of cream around the edge of the cake. Top each whirl with a chocolate curl.

11 Fill the centre with the reserved cherries. Blend the arrowroot with the reserved 45 ml (3 tbsp) syrup and boil, stirring. Brush the glaze over the cherries.

SQUIDGY CHOCOLATE MOUSSE CAKE

| 1.30* | 🍴 £ £ ✳* | 586 cals |

* plus 1 hour cooling and overnight
chilling; freeze after stage 6

Serves 8

450 g (1 lb) plain chocolate

**45 ml (3 tbsp) orange-flavoured
liqueur**

9 eggs, 5 of them separated

150 g (5 oz) caster sugar

**100 g (4 oz) unsalted butter,
softened**

**blanched julienne strips of orange
rind and grated chocolate, to
decorate**

1 Grease a 20-cm (8-inch)
spring-release tin, line with
greaseproof paper and grease the
paper.

2 Break half the chocolate into a
heatproof bowl and place over
a pan of simmering water and stir
gently until the chocolate has
melted. Stir in 15 ml (1 tbsp)
liqueur, then remove from the
heat.

3 Using an electric whisk, whisk
five egg yolks and the sugar
together until thick and creamy,
then beat in the butter a little at a
time until smooth. Beat in the
melted chocolate until smooth.

4 Whisk the five egg whites until
stiff, then fold into the chocolate mixture. Turn into the prepared tin and bake in the oven at
180°C (350°F) mark 4 for 40
minutes until risen and firm.
Leave the cake to cool in the tin
for 1 hour.

5 Make the top layer: melt the
remaining chocolate as before,
then stir in the remaining liqueur.
Remove from the heat, cool for
1–2 minutes. Separate the remaining eggs and beat the egg yolks
into the chocolate mixture. Whisk
the egg whites until stiff, then fold
into the chocolate mixture.

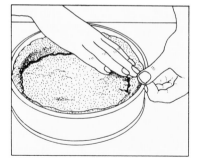

6 Press the crust down on the
baked cake with your fingers
and pour the top layer over it.
Refrigerate overnight.

7 The next day, remove the cake
carefully from the tin and put
on to a serving plate.

8 Arrange blanched strips of
orange rind around the outside
edge and decorate with grated
chocolate.

CHOCOLATE VIENNESE FINGERS

1.00* £ ✳* | 89 cals |

* plus 1 hour cooling and setting;
freeze after stage 5

Makes about 18

125 g (4 oz) butter or block
    margarine

25 g (1 oz) icing sugar

75 g (3 oz) plain chocolate

125 g (4 oz) plain flour

1.25 ml ($\frac{1}{4}$ tsp) baking powder

15 ml (1 tbsp) drinking chocolate
    powder

few drops of vanilla flavouring

1 Grease two baking sheets. Put the butter into a bowl and beat until pale and soft, then beat in the icing sugar.

2 Break 25 g (1 oz) chocolate into a heatproof bowl and place over simmering water. Stir until the chocolate is melted, then remove from heat and leave to cool for 10 minutes.

3 When the chocolate is cool, but not thick, beat it into the creamed mixture.

4 Sift in the flour, baking powder and drinking chocolate. Beat well, adding a few drops of vanilla flavouring.

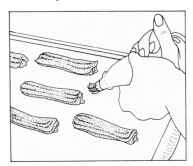

5 Spoon into a piping bag fitted with a medium star vegetable nozzle and pipe finger shapes about 7.5 cm (3 inches) long on to the prepared baking sheets, allowing room between each for the mixture to spread. Bake at 190°C (375°F) mark 5 for 15–20 minutes until crisp and pale golden. Cool on a wire rack for 30 minutes.

6 When the fingers are cold, break the remaining 50 g (2 oz) chocolate into a heatproof bowl. Stand the bowl over a pan of simmering water and stir until the chocolate has melted. Remove from the heat and dip both ends of the fingers into the melted chocolate. Leave on a wire rack for 30 minutes to set.

CHOCOLATE MERINGUE GÂTEAU

3.30* ☐ ✳* 348–464 cals

* plus 30 minutes cooling; freeze after stage 4

Serves 6–8

3 egg whites and 2 egg yolks

225 g (8 oz) caster sugar

50 g (2 oz) plain chocolate

50 g (2 oz) unsalted butter, softened

150 ml (5 fl oz) double cream

chocolate curls (see page 153), to decorate

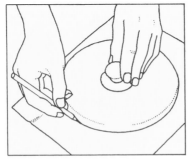

1 Using a pan lid as a guide, draw two 20-cm (8-inch) circles on non-stick paper and place on separate baking sheets.

2 Whisk the egg whites until stiff and whisk in 75 g (3 oz) sugar. Whisk again for 5 minutes until stiff. Carefully fold in another 75 g (3 oz) of the caster sugar.

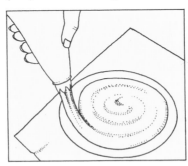

3 Spoon the mixture into a piping bag fitted with a large star nozzle and pipe the mixture on to the circles on the baking sheets. Or, using a palette knife, spread the mixture evenly.

4 Bake in the oven at 110°C (225°F) mark ¼ for about 1¾ hours or until dry. Leave to cool on the baking sheets for 30 minutes.

5 Prepare the filling for the meringues. Beat the egg yolks in a bowl. Put the remaining sugar and 45 ml (3 tbsp) water into a small pan and heat to dissolve the sugar.

6 Bring to the boil and boil to 110°C (230°F) on a sugar thermometer, or until the mixture reaches the soft ball stage. Check by plunging a teaspoonful into a bowl of iced water. It should form a ball in your fingers.

7 Pour the syrup on to the egg yolks in a steady stream, whisking all the time. Continue to whisk until thick and mousse-like.

8 Break the chocolate into a heatproof bowl and place over simmering water. Stir until the chocolate is melted then remove from the heat and leave to cool slightly for 5 minutes. Gradually beat the butter and melted chocolate into the syrup mixture.

9 Carefully peel the paper from the meringues then use the chocolate filling to sandwich the rounds together. Whip the cream until stiff, then, using a piping bag with a large star nozzle, pipe it on to the gâteau. Decorate with chocolate curls.

MARBLED CHOCOLATE RING CAKE

| 2.00* | 🍴 🍴 | £ £ | ✳* | 775 cals |

* plus 1¼ hours cooling and 1 hour setting; freeze after stage 6

Serves 8

250 g (9 oz) plain chocolate

5 ml (1 tsp) vanilla flavouring

45 ml (3 tbsp) water

350 g (12 oz) butter

225 g (8 oz) caster sugar

4 eggs, size 2, beaten

225 g (8 oz) plain flour

10 ml (2 tsp) baking powder

2.5 ml (½ tsp) salt

50 g (2 oz) ground almonds

30 ml (2 tbsp) milk

1 Grease a 1.7-litre (3-pint) ring mould. Break 50 g (2 oz) chocolate into a heatproof bowl. Add the vanilla flavouring and 15 ml (1 tbsp) water and place over simmering water. Stir until the chocolate is melted, then remove from heat and leave to cool for 10 minutes.

2 Put 225 g (8 oz) butter and the caster sugar into a bowl and beat together until pale and fluffy. Beat in the eggs one at a time.

3 Fold the flour, baking powder and salt into the creamed mixture with the ground almonds. Stir in the milk. Spoon half the mixture into base of ring mould.

4 Stir the cooled but still soft chocolate into the remaining mixture. Spoon into the tin.

5 Draw a knife through the cake mixture in a spiral. Level the surface of the mixture again.

6 Bake in the oven at 180°C (350°F) mark 4 for about 55 minutes or until a fine warmed skewer inserted in the centre comes out clean. Turn out on to a wire rack to cool for 1 hour.

7 Make the chocolate frosting. Break 150 g (5 oz) chocolate into a heatproof bowl with 30 ml (2 tbsp) water and the remaining butter. Place over simmering water and stir until the chocolate is melted, then pour over the cooled cake, working quickly to coat top and sides. Leave to set for 1 hour.

8 Melt the remaining chocolate over simmering water as before. Spoon into a greaseproof paper piping bag, snip off the tip and drizzle chocolate over the cake.

CHOCOLATE MACAROON LOG

| 2.00* | 🍴 | 477 cals |

* plus overnight chilling

Serves 10

3 egg whites, size 6

175 g (6 oz) ground almonds

275 g (10 oz) caster sugar

7.5 ml (1½ tsp) almond flavouring

100 g (4 oz) shelled hazel nuts

100 g (4 oz) plain chocolate

300 ml (10 fl oz) double cream

45 ml (3 tbsp) almond liqueur

icing sugar, cocoa, chocolate
   leaves, to decorate

1 Line two baking sheets with non-stick paper. Whisk the egg whites until stiff then fold in the ground almonds, caster sugar and almond flavouring.

2 Spoon into a piping bag fitted with a 1-cm (½-inch) plain nozzle and pipe 30 small rounds on to the prepared baking sheets, allowing room between each for the mixture to spread.

3 Bake in the oven at 180°C (350°F) mark 4 for about 20 minutes. Transfer to a wire rack for 20 minutes to cool.

4 Spread the nuts out on a baking sheet and brown in the oven at 200°C (400°F) mark 6 for 5–10 minutes. Put into a soft tea towel and rub off the skins. Chop finely, reserving two whole nuts.

5 Break the chocolate in small pieces into a heatproof bowl and place over simmering water until the chocolate is melted, then remove from heat and cool for 5 minutes.

6 Whip the cream until it holds its shape and gradually beat in the cooled chocolate, nuts and liqueur.

7 Use some of the chocolate cream to sandwich the maca-roons together.

8 Place side by side on a serving plate to form a double log. Spread chocolate cream on top and add a further layer of macaroons. Spread remaining chocolate cream over the top and sides, refrigerate overnight.

9 Dust with icing sugar and cocoa then decorate with chocolate leaves and the reserved whole hazel nuts. Serve with more whipped cream, if liked.

————— VARIATION —————

To make the hazel nut flavour more pronounced in this recipe, substitute ground, unblanched hazel nuts for the almonds when making the macaroons and omit the almond flavouring.

Cheesecakes

Creamily rich, velvety smooth, these cheesecake recipes will set your tastebuds tingling. The perfect choice for a dinner party dessert, they taste just as good at other times of day—and your family will appreciate a little bit of luxury even if there isn't a special occasion to celebrate. Bake them a cheesecake and treat them to a new taste experience.

TRADITIONAL BAKED CHEESECAKE

1.30* ⬚ ✳* 584 cals

* plus 2–3 hours cooling; freeze after cooling in stage 7

Serves 8

50 g (2 oz) self-raising flour

2.5 ml (½ tsp) baking powder

50 g (2 oz) butter, softened

275 g (10 oz) caster sugar

5 eggs, size 2

450 g (1 lb) full fat soft cheese

40 g (1½ oz) plain flour

grated rind and juice of 1 lemon

300 ml (10 fl oz) soured cream

75 g (3 oz) sultanas

pinch of freshly grated nutmeg

1 Grease a 20-cm (8-inch) round spring-release cake tin. Base-line with greaseproof paper and grease the paper.

2 Sift the self-raising flour and baking powder into a bowl. Add the butter, 50 g (2 oz) sugar and 1 egg. Mix well and beat for 2–3 minutes. Spread the sponge mixture evenly over the bottom of the prepared tin.

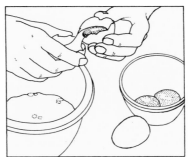

3 Separate the remaining eggs. Whisk the egg yolks with the remaining sugar until the mixture is thick and creamy.

4 Beat the cheese lightly. Add the whisked egg mixture and mix until smooth. Sift in the plain flour and stir it in, add the lemon rind and juice, half the soured cream and the sultanas and stir in.

5 Whisk the egg whites until stiff and fold into the mixture. Pour into the sponge-lined tin.

6 Bake in the oven at 170°C (325°F) mark 3 for 1 hour or until firm but still spongy to the touch. Turn off the heat and leave in the oven for 1 hour with the door ajar.

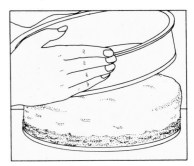

7 Remove from the oven and cool completely for 2–3 hours. Carefully remove the cheesecake from the tin. To serve, spread the remaining soured cream over the top and sprinkle with grated nutmeg.

TRADITIONAL CHEESECAKES

This cheesecake is made with a simple, unripened cheese; it is a creamy cheese made from full milk and enriched with double cream to give a high fat content. This gives the cheesecake a superbly smooth texture. The soured cream blended in during mixing adds a slight tang to the flavour. The lemon flavouring and added sultanas are traditional ingredients of a European baked cheesecake.

The cheese for this recipe is blended with eggs for a full rich texture—whisking and folding in the whites separately gives an unexpected lightness. Cheesecake is baked at a moderately low temperature to make sure that the eggs do not curdle.

HOT CHOCOLATE CHEESECAKE

| 2.45 | 🍴 🍴 | £ £ | 377–471 cals |

Serves 8–10

100 g (4 oz) unsalted butter, melted

225 g (8 oz) chocolate digestive
  biscuits, crushed

2 eggs, separated

75 g (3 oz) caster sugar

225 g (8 oz) curd cheese

40 g (1½ oz) ground or very finely
  chopped hazel nuts

150 ml (5 fl oz) double cream

25 g (1 oz) cocoa powder

10 ml (2 tsp) dark rum

icing sugar, to finish

2 Whisk the egg yolks and sugar together until thick enough to leave a trail on the surface when the whisk is lifted.

3 Whisk in the cheese, nuts, cream, cocoa powder and rum until evenly blended.

4 Whisk the egg whites until stiff, then fold into the cheese mixture. Pour into the biscuit base, then bake in the oven at 170°C (325°F) mark 3 for 1½–1¾ hours until risen.

1 Stir the melted butter into the crushed biscuits and mix well, then press into the base and 4 cm (1½ inches) up the sides of a 20-cm (8-inch) loose-bottomed cake tin. Refrigerate for 30 minutes.

5 Remove carefully from the tin, sift the icing sugar over the top to coat lightly and serve immediately while still hot.

UNRIPENED CHEESES

Cheesecakes are always made from unripened cheeses. These may be full fat soft cheese (see page 69), curd cheese as here, or cottage cheese. Curd cheese is made from full milk and has the most pronounced 'cheesy' flavour. Its texture is slightly grainy when compared with the cream-enriched full fat soft cheese. Cottage cheese is lighter than either, made from skimmed milk. The texture of cottage cheese is lumpy, the flavour mild and there is often a good deal of whey left in the cheese, making it rather moist.

This recipe is not as rich in fat as the Traditional Baked Cheesecake but the flavour is more pronounced. Combined with chocolate, dark rum and nuts, curd cheese packs a powerful punch! Unusually, this cheesecake is eaten warm, straight from the oven. Remove it very carefully from the baking tin, so as not to break the biscuit crumb case. You will find that small portions are quite enough for most people!

COFFEE CHEESECAKE

| 1.00* | ✳ | 380 cals |

* plus 2–3 hours chilling

Serves 8

50 g (2 oz) butter, melted

175 g (6 oz) gingernut biscuits, finely crushed

15 ml (1 tbsp) gelatine

45 ml (3 tbsp) cold water

15 ml (1 tbsp) instant coffee powder

30 ml (2 tbsp) coffee-flavoured liqueur

300 ml (½ pint) boiling water

150 g (5 oz) soft brown sugar

450 g (1 lb) curd cheese

300 ml (10 fl oz) whipping cream

coffee beans, to decorate

1 Lightly oil a 20-cm (8-inch) loose-bottomed deep cake tin or spring-release cake tin.

2 Stir the butter into the crushed biscuits. Press firmly into the base of the tin. Refrigerate for 30 minutes until set.

3 Sprinkle the gelatine on to the cold water. Leave to soak for 10 minutes.

4 Stir the coffee and coffee liqueur into the boiling water. Add the soaked gelatine, stirring until dissolved. Stir in the sugar.

5 Put the coffee mixture and curd cheese into a blender and work until just smooth. Leave until beginning to set then lightly whip the cream and fold half into the cheese mixture.

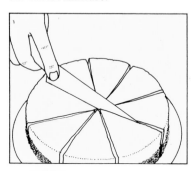

6 Turn the mixture into the prepared tin and refrigerate for 2–3 hours or until set. When set, remove from the tin. To serve, cut into eight, pipe a cream whirl on top of each slice and decorate with coffee beans.

ALTERNATIVE DECORATIONS

For even better effect, buy sugar coffee beans, available from high-class confectioners. Alternatively, thin chocolate leaves or squares would look attractive and taste good.

QUICK CHERRY CHEESECAKE

1.00* ✳ 699–1049 cals

* plus 2–3 hours chilling

Serves 4–6

65 g (2½ oz) unsalted butter, melted

150 g (5 oz) digestive biscuits, crushed

225 g (8 oz) full fat soft cheese

2.5 ml (½ tsp) vanilla flavouring

60 ml (4 tbsp) icing sugar, sifted

300 ml (10 fl oz) double cream

400-g (14-oz) can cherry pie filling

1 Stir the melted butter into the crushed biscuits and mix well, then press into the base and sides of a 22-cm (8½-inch) fluted flan dish. Refrigerate for 30 minutes.

2 Put the cheese into a bowl and beat until soft and creamy, then beat in the vanilla flavouring and icing sugar.

3 Whip the cream until it holds its shape, then fold into the cheese until evenly blended.

4 Spoon the mixture into the biscuit base and level the surface. Refrigerate for 30 minutes.

5 Spoon the pie filling over the top of the cheesecake. Refrigerate for 2–3 hours to set.

GOOSEBERRY CHEESECAKE

2.30* ⬜ ✳* 664 cals

* plus 30 minutes cooling and 1–2 hours chilling; freeze after stage 8

Serves 6

450 g (1 lb) gooseberries, topped and tailed

75 ml (5 tbsp) water

125 g (4 oz) caster sugar

75 g (3 oz) shelled hazel nuts

75 g (3 oz) butter

175 g (6 oz) digestive biscuits, finely crushed

125 g (4 oz) cottage cheese

225 g (8 oz) full fat soft cheese

150 ml (5 fl oz) double cream

2 eggs, separated

15 ml (1 tbsp) lemon juice

7.5 ml (1½ tsp) gelatine

1 Put the gooseberries into a pan with 60 ml (4 tbsp) water and 75 g (3 oz) caster sugar. Cover and cook slowly for 20 minutes until the fruit becomes mushy.

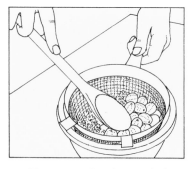

2 To remove the pips, push the fruit through a nylon sieve into a clean bowl and let the purée cool for 30 minutes.

3 Roughly chop 50 g (2 oz) hazel nuts and fry gently in the butter until golden, stir in the finely crushed digestive biscuits.

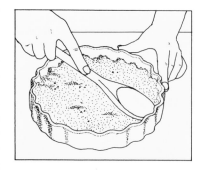

4 Press the digestive biscuit mixture into the base of a 24-cm (9½-inch) deep fluted flan dish. Refrigerate for 30 minutes to 1 hour to set.

5 Sieve the cottage cheese into a large bowl and gradually beat in the soft cheese followed by the cream to give a smooth consistency.

6 Whisk the egg yolks and remaining caster sugar until thick enough to leave a trail on the surface when the whisk is lifted. Stir into the cheese mixture.

7 Spoon the lemon juice into a small bowl with the remaining water and sprinkle in the gelatine. Leave to soak for 10 minutes. Stand the bowl over a pan of gently simmering water until the gelatine dissolves then stir into the cheese mixture with half the fruit purée.

8 Whisk one egg white until stiff and fold into the mixture then spoon into the lined flan dish. Refrigerate for 1–2 hours.

9 Meanwhile, brown the remaining nuts: spread them out on a baking sheet and brown in the oven at 200°C (400°F) mark 6 for 5–10 minutes. Put into a soft tea towel and rub off the skins. Chop and use to decorate. Serve remaining purée separately.

MINI GRAPE CHEESECAKES

1.30* ✳* 247 cals

* plus 30 minutes cooling and 1 hour chilling; freeze after stage 5

Makes 24

275 g (10 oz) plain flour plus 10 ml (2 tsp)

pinch of salt

175 g (6 oz) butter or block margarine, cut into pieces

75 g (3 oz) caster sugar

about 60 ml (4 tbsp) water

225 g (8 oz) full fat soft cheese

2 eggs, beaten

finely grated rind and juice of $\frac{1}{2}$ lemon

175 g (6 oz) black grapes, halved and seeded

150 ml (5 fl oz) whipping cream, whipped

1 Put 275 g (10 oz) flour and the salt into a bowl. Rub in the butter with the fingertips until the mixture resembles breadcrumbs. Stir in 50 g (2 oz) sugar, and water to mix to a smooth dough.

2 Roll out the dough on a lightly floured surface and cut out twelve 7.5-cm (3-inch) circles using a fluted pastry cutter. Use to line twenty-four deep patty tins.

3 Cook the pastry cases 'blind' (see page 147) in the oven at 200°C (400°F) mark 6 for 10 minutes, remove the foil and beans, then return to the oven for a further 5 minutes.

4 Meanwhile, make the filling. In a bowl, beat the soft cheese, eggs, the remaining sugar and flour and the lemon rind and juice until evenly mixed.

5 Pour the filling into the pastry cases. Lower the oven temperature to 150°C (300°F) mark 2 and bake the cheesecakes for 15 minutes until the fillings are set. Cool on a wire rack for 30 minutes then refrigerate for at least 1 hour.

6 Just before serving, decorate the top of each cheesecake with the grapes and piped whipped cream.

LEMON CHEESECAKE

1.00* ▯ ✳* 375–500 cals

* plus 2–3 hours chilling; freeze after stage 7

Serves 6

1$\frac{1}{2}$ packets of lemon jelly

60 ml (4 tbsp) water

2 eggs, separated

300 ml ($\frac{1}{2}$ pint) milk

grated rind of 2 lemons

90 ml (6 tbsp) lemon juice

450 g (1 lb) cottage cheese

65 g (2$\frac{1}{2}$ oz) caster sugar

150 ml (5 fl oz) double cream

100 g (4 oz) digestive biscuits, finely crushed

50 g (2 oz) butter, melted

fresh lemon slices, to decorate

1 Lightly oil a 20-cm (8-inch) spring-release cake tin fitted with a tubular base.

2 Put the jelly and water into a small pan and warm gently over a low heat, stirring until dissolved. Remove from the heat.

3 Beat together the egg yolks and milk, pour on to the jelly, stir and return to the heat for a few minutes without boiling. Remove from the heat and add the lemon rind and juice.

4 Sieve the cottage cheese and stir into the jelly or put jelly and cottage cheese into an electric blender or food processor and blend to form a smooth purée. Turn the mixture into a bowl and leave to cool for 10 minutes.

5 Whisk the egg whites until stiff, add 15 g ($\frac{1}{2}$ oz) sugar and whisk again until stiff. Fold into the cooled cheese mixture.

6 Whip the cream until stiff and fold into the mixture. Turn into the cake tin.

7 Mix together the biscuit crumbs and remaining sugar and stir in the melted butter. Use to cover the cheesecake mixture, pressing it on lightly. Refrigerate for 2–3 hours or overnight. To serve, turn cheesecake out and decorate with slices of lemon.

CHEESECAKE

995 cals

freeze after

...ed
...late
...ely

...oconut

...uice

...t cheese

...ice
...cream
...sliced

5 Stand the bowl over a pan of hot water and heat gently until dissolved. Leave the gelatine mixture to cool for 5 minutes.

6 Beat the soft cheese and sugar until smooth, then beat in the egg yolks and lemon juice. Stir in the mango flesh and gelatine mixture. Lightly whip the cream and fold into the mixture.

7 Whisk the egg whites until stiff and carefully fold into the cheese mixture. Pour into the prepared tin and place in the refrigerator for 3–4 hours until firm.

8 To serve, carefully remove the cheesecake from the tin. Decorate with the sliced kiwi fruit.

1 Lightly oil a 22-cm (8½-inch) spring-release cake tin. Base-line with greaseproof paper and grease the paper.

2 Stir the melted butter into the biscuit crumbs and coconut. Mix well together, then press into the prepared tin and chill in the refrigerator for 30 minutes.

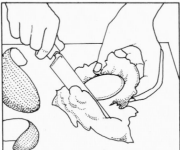

3 Peel the mangoes and cut the flesh from the flat oval stone. Discard the stone.

4 Roughly chop or mash the flesh. Put the orange juice into a bowl and sprinkle in the gelatine. Leave to soak for 2–3 minutes until softened.

TROPICAL FRUIT

The mango is a fruit of ancient Asian origin, though it is now grown in many parts of the world with a tropical or sub-tropical climate. The best varieties are sweet, aromatic and juicy, with a distinctive and uniquely delicious flavour. Lesser varieties, or less ripe fruit, are not so tasty and are inclined to be fibrous—don't be put off if these are the type you first experience. The less tasty fruit make good chutneys and preserves for serving with cold meats or cheese; mango chutney is a traditional condiment with curry. Canned mangoes are available, but are inclined to be over-sweet, loosing the slight acidity of their natural flavour.

Kiwi fruit, also known as Chinese gooseberries, are less variable. Originating in China, many are now grown in New Zealand and in other warm countries. Peel off the thin, hairy, brown skin and the entire fruit can be eaten. It is highly decorative—a fresh light green colour with a cluster of dark seeds forming a circle round the soft core—and the flavour is refreshing.

Special Occasion Cakes

Even if you never think of making a cake at any other time of year, there are certain special occasions when you feel like pulling out all the stops. The cakes in this chapter are designed for traditional celebrations — from Christmas and New Year through to Mother's Day, Easter and Harvest Festival. And Croquembouche, the French wedding cake, is the pièce de résistance!

YULE LOG

| 1.30* | ⊟ | £ | ❄* | 396 cals |

* plus 1½ hours chilling; freeze after stage 7

Serves 8

3 eggs

100 g (4 oz) caster sugar

100 g (4 oz) plain flour

15 ml (1 tbsp) hot water

caster sugar

1 quantity chocolate crème au beurre (see page 154)

icing sugar, to decorate

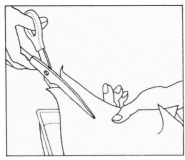

1 Grease a 30 × 20 cm (12 × 8 inch) Swiss roll tin. Line the tin with greaseproof paper and grease the paper.

2 Put the eggs and sugar into a large bowl and whisk until thick enough to leave a trail on the surface of the mixture when the whisk is lifted.

3 Sift half the flour over the mixture and fold in very lightly with a metal spoon. Sift and fold in the remaining flour, then lightly stir in the hot water.

4 Pour the mixture into the prepared tin. Bake in the oven at 220°C (425°F) mark 7 for 8–12 minutes until golden brown, well risen and firm to the touch.

5 Meanwhile, place a sheet of greaseproof paper over a tea towel wrung out in hot water. Dredge the paper with a little caster sugar.

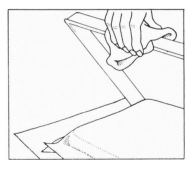

6 Quickly turn out the cake on to the greaseproof paper and trim off the crusty edges with a sharp knife.

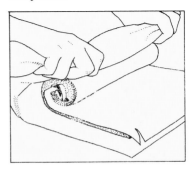

7 Roll up the cake with the greaseproof paper inside it. Leave to cool on a wire rack for about 30 minutes.

8 When cold, unroll the cake carefully, removing the paper. Spread one third of the buttercream over the surface and re-roll. Refrigerate for 30 minutes until the roll is firm.

9 Coat with the remaining buttercream and mark lines with a fork to resemble tree bark.

10 Chill for 1 hour before serving. Dust lightly with icing sugar and decorate with a sprig of real or artificial holly.

—— VARIATION ——

For a Chestnut log replace the buttercream with a 440-g (15½-oz) can of sweetened chestnut pureé.

BLACK BUN

4.00* ∐ £ £ 391 cals

* plus 1–2 hours cooling

Serves 12

shortcrust pastry made with 225 g
  (8 oz) plain flour (see page 147)

225 g (8 oz) plain flour

5 ml (1 tsp) ground cinnamon

5 ml (1 tsp) ground ginger

5 ml (1 tsp) ground allspice

5 ml (1 tsp) cream of tartar

5 ml (1 tsp) bicarbonate of soda

450 g (1 lb) seedless raisins

450 g (1 lb) currants

50 g (2 oz) chopped mixed peel

100 g (4 oz) chopped almonds

100 g (4 oz) soft dark brown sugar

1 egg, beaten

150 ml ($\frac{1}{4}$ pint) whisky

about 60 ml (4 tbsp) milk

beaten egg, to glaze

1 Grease a 20-cm (8-inch) round
cake tin. Roll out two-thirds of
the pastry on a lightly floured
working surface into a round about
35 cm (14 inches) in diameter.

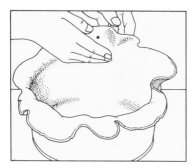

2 Line the prepared tin with the
pastry, making sure it over-
hangs the sides.

3 Sift together the flour, spices,
cream of tartar and bicarbonate
of soda. Mix in the raisins,
currants, peel, almonds and sugar.

4 Add the egg, whisky and milk
and stir until the mixture is
evenly moistened. Pack the filling
into the pastry case and fold the
top of the pastry over.

5 On a lightly floured surface,
roll out the remaining dough
to a 20-cm (8-inch) round. Moisten
the edges of the pastry case, put
the pastry round on top and seal
the edges firmly together.

6 With a skewer, make four or
five holes right down to the
bottom of the cake, then prick all
over the top with a fork and brush
with beaten egg.

7 Bake in the oven at 180°C
(350°F) mark 4 for $2\frac{1}{2}$–3 hours
or until a fine warmed skewer inserted in the centre comes out
clean. Check near the end of cooking time and cover with several
layers of greaseproof paper, if it is
overbrowning. Turn out on to a
wire rack and leave for 1–2 hours
to cool completely, before serving.

CROQUEMBOUCHE

2.00* ☐ ☐ £ £ ✳

519–623 cals

* plus 1 hour cooling

Serves 25–30

treble quantity choux pastry (see page 149)

1 quantity pâte sucrée (see page 146)

quadruple quantity crème pâtissière (see page 155) or 900 ml (30 fl oz) double cream, 300 ml (10 fl oz) single cream and 90 ml (6 tbsp) caster sugar

1.1 kg (2¼ lb) sugar

900 ml (1½ pints) water

crystallised rose petals and violets, to decorate

1 Dampen three baking sheets with water. Put the choux pastry into a piping bag fitted with a medium plain nozzle and pipe about sixty 2-cm (¾-inch) buns on to the baking sheets.

2 Bake in the oven at 200°C (400°F) mark 6 for 20–25 minutes until well risen and golden brown. Make a small slit in the side of each bun to release the steam, then transfer to a wire rack and leave for 30 minutes to cool.

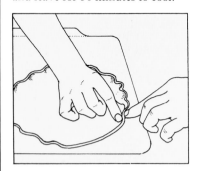

3 Roll out the pâte sucrée on a lightly floured working surface to a 22-cm (8½-inch) round. Place on a baking sheet, crimp the edge and prick all over with a fork.

4 Bake in the oven at 180°C (350°F) mark 4 for 20 minutes until light golden brown. Cool for 30 minutes on a wire rack then transfer to a cake stand; use a highly ornamental one for a very special occasion.

5 Fill each choux bun with a little crème pâtissière. Or whip the double and single cream together until stiff, fold in the caster sugar and use to fill the buns.

6 Make the caramel. Put one third of the granulated sugar with one third of the water into a heavy based saucepan.

7 Heat gently to dissolve the sugar and then bring to the boil and boil to 143°C–154°C (290°F–310°F) on a sugar thermometer or until the mixture reaches the hard crack stage. Remove from the heat and place the pan on a mat so it is tilted.

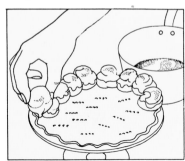

8 Dip one side of the filled choux buns into the caramel. Arrange around the edge of the pâte sucrée base, sticking the edges together.

9 Fill the centre with more caramel choux buns. When the first layer is completed, make another on top.

10 Continue in this way, building up into a cone shape and packing the buns loosely. Make more caramel as necessary.

11 When the cone is completed, make up more caramel using the remaining sugar and water and drizzle over the Croquembouche. Decorate with crystallised rose petals and violets.

SPUN SUGAR

This can be used to decorate the Croquembouche, a traditional French wedding cake.

Dissolve 225 g (8 oz) sugar in 150 ml (¼ pint) water and boil to 150°C (300°F). Quickly place pan in cold water; once the sugar has stopped boiling, remove the pan from the water bath and allow to cool a little. Hold two forks together facing each other and dip into the sugar; swing them freely around the Croquembouche and the sugar should fall off the forks in long silvery threads, which harden immediately.

STOLLEN

| 2.00* | ⬚ ⬚ | £ £ | 145–218 cals |

* plus 1–2 hours cooling
Serves 8–12

15 g (½ oz) fresh yeast or 7.5 ml
  (1½ tsp) dried yeast plus a pinch
  of sugar

100 ml (4 fl oz) tepid milk

225 g (8 oz) strong plain flour

1.25 ml (¼ tsp) salt

25 g (1 oz) block margarine

grated rind of 1 small lemon

50 g (2 oz) chopped mixed peel

50 g (2 oz) currants

50 g (2 oz) sultanas

25 g (1 oz) blanched almonds,
  chopped

½ a beaten egg

icing sugar, to dredge

1 Grease a large baking sheet.
Crumble the fresh yeast into a
bowl and cream with the milk
until smooth. If using the dried
yeast and sugar, sprinkle the mixture into the milk and leave in a
warm place for 15 minutes until
the surface is frothy.

2 Put the flour and salt into a
bowl and rub in the margarine.
Add the lemon, fruit and nuts.
Add the yeast mixture and beaten
egg and mix thoroughly to a soft
dough.

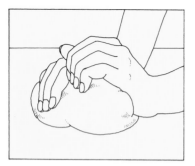

3 Turn on to a lightly floured
working surface and knead for
about 10 minutes until smooth.

4 Cover with a clean cloth and
leave to rise in a warm place
for about 1 hour until doubled.

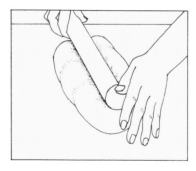

5 Knead the dough for 2–3
minutes, then roll into an oval
shape about 23 × 18 cm (9 × 7
inches). Mark a line lengthways
with the rolling pin.

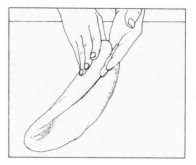

6 Carefully fold the dough in
half along the marked line.
Place on the baking sheet, cover
with a clean cloth and leave in a
warm place for about 40 minutes
until doubled in size.

7 Bake in the oven at 200°C
(400°F) mark 6 for about 30
minutes until well risen and golden
brown. Transfer to a wire rack to
cool. To serve, dredge all over
with icing sugar.

HARVEST CAKE

3.45* ⬚ £ £ ✳* 605 cals

* plus 2–3 hours cooling; freeze after stage 7

Serves 10

175 g (6 oz) butter or block margarine
175 g (6 oz) dark soft brown sugar
3 eggs, beaten
225 g (8 oz) plain flour
5 ml (1 tsp) baking powder
5 ml (1 tsp) ground cinnamon
5 ml (1 tsp) freshly grated nutmeg
pinch of salt
225 g (8 oz) sultanas
100 g (4 oz) seedless raisins
100 g (4 oz) dried apricots, chopped
175 g (6 oz) Brazil nuts, chopped
60 ml (4 tbsp) black treacle
finely grated rind and juice of 1 lemon
about 30 ml (2 tbsp) brandy
300 g (11 oz) marzipan
icing sugar
15–30 ml (1–2 tbsp) apricot jam
marzipan fruits (see below)

1 Grease a 20-cm (8-inch) round cake tin. Line with greaseproof paper and grease the paper.

2 Put the butter and sugar into a bowl and beat together until pale and fluffy. Beat in the eggs a little at a time.

3 Sift the flour with the baking powder, spices and salt and fold into the creamed mixture. Stir in the dried fruit and nuts, black treacle, lemon rind and juice until evenly mixed.

4 Add enough brandy to give a soft, dropping consistency. (Add more brandy or a little milk if the mixture is too stiff.)

5 Turn the mixture into the prepared tin and make a slight hollow in the centre with the back of a metal spoon. Bake at 170°C (325°F) mark 3 for 1 hour.

6 Cover with foil and lower the oven to 150°C (300°F) mark 2. Cook for a further 2 hours or until a fine warmed skewer inserted in the centre comes out clean.

7 Leave the cake to cool in the tin for 2–3 hours, then turn out and peel off the lining paper.

8 Knead the marzipan on a surface lightly dusted with icing sugar. Roll out to a circle slightly larger than the diameter of the cake.

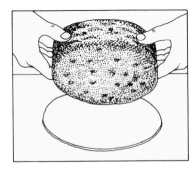

9 Brush the top of the cake with the apricot jam, then press the cake gently on to the marzipan, jam-side down.

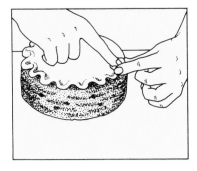

10 Turn the cake the right way up, trim off the excess marzipan with a sharp knife, then crimp the edge and decorate with marzipan fruits.

MARZIPAN FRUITS
Mould marzipan into fruit shapes. Paint with diluted food colouring; use cloves for stalks.

CHRISTMAS CAKE

4.15* 🎩 £ £ 391 cals

* Make cake at least one month before required; icing times vary; see page 158 for decorating details

Serves 30

225 g (8 oz) currants
225 g (8 oz) sultanas
225 g (8 oz) seedless raisins, chopped
100 g (4 oz) chopped mixed peel
100 g (4 oz) glacé cherries, halved
50 g (2 oz) nibbed almonds
225 g (8 oz) plain flour
pinch of salt
2.5 ml ($\frac{1}{2}$ tsp) ground mace
2.5 ml ($\frac{1}{2}$ tsp) ground cinnamon
225 g (8 oz) butter
225 g (8 oz) soft dark brown sugar
finely grated rind of 1 lemon
4 eggs, size 2, beaten
30 ml (2 tbsp) brandy

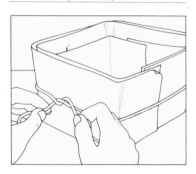

1 Grease a round 20.5-cm (8-inch) or square 18-cm (7-inch) cake tin, using a double thickness of greaseproof paper, and tie a double band of brown paper round the outside.

2 Mix the currants, sultanas, raisins, mixed peel, cherries and nuts. Sift the flour, salt and spices into a bowl.

3 Cream the butter, dark brown sugar and grated lemon rind together until the mixture is pale and fluffy. Add the eggs, a little at a time, beating well after each addition to prevent curdling.

4 Fold half the sifted flour mixture lightly into the mixture with a metal spoon, then fold in the rest and add the brandy. Finally, fold in the fruit.

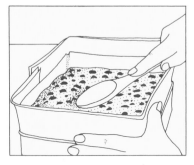

5 Turn the mixture into the prepared tin, spreading it evenly and making sure there are no air pockets. Make a hollow in the centre with the back of a spoon.

6 Stand the tin on a layer of newspaper or brown paper in the oven and bake at 150°C (300°F) mark 2 for about $3\frac{3}{4}$ hours. Cover the top with several layers of greaseproof paper after $1\frac{1}{2}$ hours to avoid overbrowning.

7 When the cake is cooked, leave to cool in the tin and then turn out on to a wire rack.

8 To store, wrap the cake in several layers of greaseproof paper, then in foil and put in an airtight tin. To decorate the Christmas cake, see the designs on page 158.

Dessert Cakes

Everyone looks forward
to the dessert course, and
a homemade cake or
pastry never fails to
impress. Your guests are
bound to appreciate the
effort—and skill—you've
put into making them.

The flavour of home-
made cakes and pastries
far surpasses any fancy
pâtisserie you can buy,
so dip into this chapter
and you'll be amazed how
clever you can be.

ALMOND RUM PAVLOVA

3.00* ▯ £ £ ❄* 367 cals

* plus 1 hour cooling and 20 minutes chilling; freeze after stage 6

Serves 8

| 75 g (3 oz) ground almonds |
| 4 eggs, separated |
| 250 g (9 oz) caster sugar |
| 10 ml (2 tsp) cornflour |
| 10 ml (2 tsp) white vinegar |
| 16 flaked almonds |
| 15 ml (1 tbsp) dark rum |
| 50 g (2 oz) unsalted butter |
| 150 ml (5 fl oz) double cream |
| 225 g (8 oz) raspberries |

1 Spread the ground almonds out on a baking sheet and brown in the oven at 200°C (400°F) mark 6 for 5–10 minutes. Remove from the oven and leave for about 15 minutes to cool.

2 Line a large baking sheet with non-stick paper. Lower the oven to 150°C (300°F) mark 2.

3 Whisk the egg whites until stiff. Add 100 g (4 oz) sugar, the cornflour and vinegar. Whisk again until very stiff and shiny. Fold in a further 100 g (4 oz) sugar and the ground almonds.

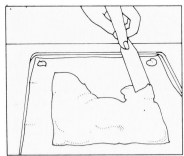

4 With a palette knife, spread one third of the meringue in a 20-cm (8-inch) square on the non-stick paper.

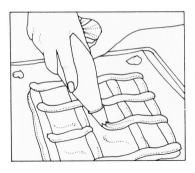

5 Spoon the remaining meringue into a piping bag fitted with a large star nozzle. Pipe lines to make a square at each corner of the meringue and then pipe a square in the centre to form nine boxes. Decorate with flaked almonds.

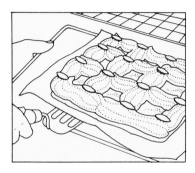

6 Put into the oven and immediately lower it to 140°C (275°F) mark 1. Bake for about 1½ hours or until well dried out. Slide on to a wire rack and cool.

7 Put the egg yolks, rum and remaining sugar into a bowl. Melt the butter gently in a small pan and pour over the egg yolks, whisking constantly until thick.

8 Lightly whip the double cream until it just holds its shape and fold into the egg mixture. When the meringue is cold, carefully peel off the paper and place the meringue on a flat plate.

9 Spoon the cream into the meringue boxes and decorate with the raspberries. Refrigerate for 20 minutes before serving.

PINEAPPLE GRIESTORTE

2.00* ⊟ f 280–373 cals

* includes 30 minutes standing time

Serves 6–8

3 eggs, separated

125 g (4 oz) caster sugar

376-g (13¼-oz) can pineapple pieces, drained and juice reserved

75 g (3 oz) semolina

300 ml (10 fl oz) whipping cream

100 g (4 oz) chopped mixed nuts, toasted

1 Grease a 20-cm (8-inch) round cake tin. Base-line with grease-proof paper and grease the paper.

2 Whisk the egg yolks and sugar in a bowl until pale and really thick. Stir in 30 ml (2 tbsp) of the reserved pineapple juice together with the semolina.

3 Whisk the egg whites until stiff, then gently fold into the yolks and sugar mixture.

4 Turn into the prepared tin. Bake in the oven at 180°C (350°F) mark 4 for about 40 minutes or until the sponge springs back when pressed lightly with a finger and has shrunk away a little from the tin. Turn out on to a wire rack and leave 30 minutes to cool.

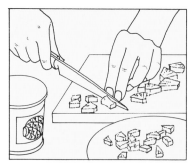

5 Roughly chop the pineapple pieces. Lightly whip the cream. Split the cake in half and fill with half the cream and half the pineapple. Spread a little of the cream around the sides and top of the cake and press the nuts on the side. Pipe the remaining cream in whirls and decorate with pineapple.

APPLE HAZEL NUT GENOESE

| 1.15* | £ | ✳* | 450 cals |

* plus 1–2 hours cooling and 2–3 hours standing time; freeze after stage 3

Serves 6

3 eggs

100 g (4 oz) caster sugar

50 g (2 oz) plain flour

15 ml (1 tbsp) cornflour

25 g (1 oz) ground hazel nuts

75 g (3 oz) butter, melted and cooled

90 ml (6 tbsp) apple jelly

seven-minute frosting (see page 155) using 30 ml (2 tbsp) thick unsweetened apple purée instead of water

1 Grease two 18-cm (7-inch) straight-sided sandwich tins. Base-line with greaseproof paper and grease the paper.

2 Whisk the eggs and caster sugar in a bowl until very thick. Sift in the flour and cornflour and add hazel nuts, then fold in butter.

3 Turn into the prepared tins and bake in the oven at 180°C (350°F) mark 4 for about 25 minutes or until the sponge springs back when pressed lightly with a finger and has shrunk away a little from the tin. Turn out on to a wire rack and leave 1–2 hours to cool.

4 Sandwich the layers with apple jelly and prepare the seven-minute frosting.

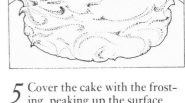

5 Cover the cake with the frosting, peaking up the surface. Leave for 2–3 hours before serving to allow the frosting to firm up.

COFFEE PRALINE GATEAU

| 1.30* | 🍳 £ £ ✳* | 350 cals |

* plus 2–4 hours cooling; freeze after
stage 4

Serves 6

2 eggs, size 2

100 g (4 oz) caster sugar

50 g (2 oz) plain flour

15 ml (1 tbsp) coffee essence

25 g (1 oz) blanched almonds

150 ml (5 fl oz) double cream

30 ml (2 tbsp) coffee-flavoured
   liqueur

icing sugar, for dusting

25 ml (5 tsp) instant coffee powder

7.5 ml (1½ tsp) arrowroot

170-g (6-oz) can evaporated milk

30 ml (2 tbsp) soft light brown
   sugar

1 Grease a 20-cm (8-inch) round
cake tin. Base-line with greaseproof paper and grease the paper.
Dust with caster sugar and flour.

2 Put eggs into a deep bowl with
75 g (3 oz) caster sugar and
whisk vigorously until the mixture
is very thick and light and leaves
a trail. If hand mixing, whisk
the mixture over a saucepan of
simmering water.

3 Sift the flour evenly over surface of the egg mixture and
fold in lightly until no traces of
flour remain. Lightly fold in the
coffee essence.

4 Turn into the prepared tin and
bake at once in the oven at
180°C (350°F) mark 4 for about 30
minutes or until the sponge springs
back when pressed lightly with a
finger and has shrunk away a little
from the tin. Turn out on to a wire
rack and leave for 1–2 hours.

5 Meanwhile, make the praline.
Oil a baking sheet. Put the
remaining caster sugar into a small
frying pan with the blanched almonds and heat gently until the
sugar dissolves and caramelises.

6 Pour the praline on to the prepared baking sheet and leave
for 10–15 minutes to cool and
harden.

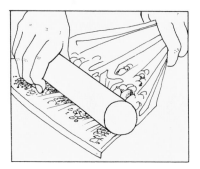

7 When cold, grind or crush with
end of a rolling pin in a strong
bowl. Whip the cream until it
holds its shape then whisk in the
liqueur and fold in three-quarters
of praline (ground nut mixture).

8 Split the sponge in half and
sandwich with the cream. Dust
the top with icing sugar and decorate with praline. Refrigerate for
1–2 hours.

9 Make the coffee sauce. In a
small pan, mix the coffee
powder and arrowroot to a smooth
paste with a little water then make
up to 150 ml (¼ pint) with more
water. Add the evaporated milk
and brown sugar and bring slowly
to the boil, stirring. Bubble for 1
minute. Serve warm.

MILLE FEUILLES

1.45*	f	436 cals*

* plus 1 hour setting; 517 cals with double cream

Makes 6

212-g (7½-oz) packet frozen puff
   pastry, thawed, or ¼ quantity
   puff pastry (see page 148)

100 g (4 oz) raspberry jam

1 quantity crème pâtissière (see
   page 155) or 300 ml (10 fl oz)
   double cream, whipped

red food colouring

1 Dampen a baking sheet. Roll
out the pastry on a lightly
floured working surface into a rectangle measuring 25 × 23 cm
(10 × 9 inches) and place on baking
sheet. Prick all over with a fork.

2 Bake in the oven at 220°C
(425°F) mark 7 for 10 minutes,
until well risen and golden brown.
Transfer to a wire rack and leave
for 30 minutes to cool.

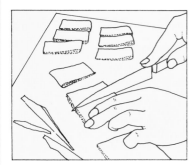

3 When cold, trim the pastry
edges, cut in half lengthways
and cut each half across into six
slices. Spread half with raspberry
jam, then cover with the crème
pâtissière or cream.

4 Spread jam on the bases of
the remaining pastry pieces
and place on top of the first layers.

5 Make 175 g (6 oz) glacé icing
(see page 154). Mix 15 ml (1
tbsp) icing with a few drops of red
colouring. Set aside. Spread remaining white icing over pastries.

6 Pour the pink icing into a
greaseproof paper piping bag.
Cut off the tip and carefully pipe
fine pink lines 1 cm (½ inch) apart
on top of the white icing, across
each pastry.

7 Draw a skewer down the
length of the mille feuilles at
1-cm (½-inch) intervals to make a
'feathering' design. Leave for 1
hour to set.

VARIATION

You can, of course, vary the
flavour of the jam filling—strawberry, blackberry or blackcurrant
would be equally delicious. And
instead of pink icing, you could
add a little coffee essence to the
glacé icing.

BAKLAVA

1.00* £ 223 cals

*plus 1–2 hours cooling

Makes 20

225 g (8 oz) shelled walnuts, ground

50 g (2 oz) light soft brown sugar

2.5 ml ($\frac{1}{2}$ tsp) ground cinnamon

450-g (1-lb) packet phyllo or strudel pastry

150 g (5 oz) butter, melted

175 g (6 oz) clear honey, warmed

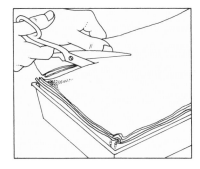

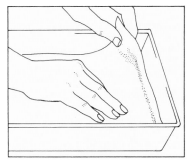

1 Grease a 24 × 18 cm (9$\frac{1}{2}$ × 7 inch) roasting tin. Mix the walnuts, sugar and cinnamon together in a bowl. Halve each sheet of pastry to measure a 25-cm (10-inch) square.

2 Fit one sheet of pastry into the bottom of the tin, allowing it to come up the sides, and brush with melted butter. Repeat with five more pastry sheets. Sprinkle with 50 g (2 oz) of the nut mixture.

3 Repeat stage 2 four more times to produce five layers of walnut mixture. Top with remaining pastry and trim sheets to fit tin.

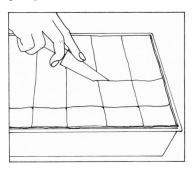

4 Mark the surface of the pastry into 20 squares with the tip of a sharp knife.

5 Bake in the oven at 220°C (425°F) mark 7 for 15 minutes, then at 180°C (350°F) mark 4 for 10–15 minutes, until golden brown. Meanwhile warm the honey in a saucepan over a low heat, spoon over the cooked baklava, and leave to cool in the tin for 1–2 hours. Cut out the marked squares.

—— VARIATION ——

Replace the phyllo pastry with 368-g (13-oz) packet bought puff pastry. Cut into six equal pieces and roll out very thinly to a 24 × 18 cm (9$\frac{1}{2}$ × 7$\frac{1}{2}$ inch) rectangle. Layer the pastry with the walnut mixture as above, using only 50 g (2 oz) of melted butter. Bake and finish as above.

HAZEL NUT APPLE SHORTCAKES

| 1.20* | 🗄 £ £ ✳* | 482 cals |

* plus about 2½ hours chilling; freeze shortcake and filling separately

Serves 6

75 g (3 oz) shelled hazel nuts

100 g (4 oz) butter, softened

75 g (3 oz) soft light brown sugar

100 g (4 oz) plain flour

700 g (1½ lb) eating apples

finely grated rind of ½ lemon

15 ml (1 tbsp) lemon juice

30 ml (2 tbsp) sugar

30 ml (2 tbsp) orange-flavoured liqueur

icing sugar

150 ml (5 fl oz) whipping cream

apple slices, to decorate

1 Spread the hazel nuts out on a baking sheet and brown in the oven at 200°C (400°F) mark 6 for 10 minutes. Put into a tea towel and rub off skins. Chop finely.

2 Put 75 g (3 oz) of the butter into a bowl and beat until pale and soft, then gradually beat in the brown sugar. Fold in the chopped nuts and flour until evenly blended; knead well until smooth.

3 Using the heel of the hand, pat half the mixture out to a 20-cm (8-inch) round on a baking sheet; crimp the edges. Pat out second piece in same way. Chill both for 15–20 minutes.

4 Bake at 180°C (350°F) mark 4 for about 20 minutes or until golden brown.

5 Meanwhile, peel, core and roughly chop the apples. Melt the remaining butter in a small pan, add the apples with the lemon rind and juice and the sugar. Cover the pan tightly and simmer for 15–20 minutes, or until apples are tender.

6 Mash or beat the apples until smooth, stir in the liqueur then leave for about 1 hour to cool.

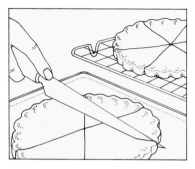

7 When the pastry is baked, immediately cut the rounds into six wedges each; ease on to wire racks and leave for 20 minutes to cool.

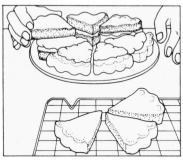

8 Place one round of wedges on a flat plate. Spread cooled apple mixture over shortcake. Top with the remaining wedges, making sure the wedges line up. Refrigerate for 2 hours. Dust with icing sugar. Lightly whip the cream and use to decorate the cake with the apple slices. Serve remaining cream separately.

PALMIERS

| 1.00 | £ ✳* | 323 cals |

* after stage 6

Makes 12

368-g (13-oz) packet frozen puff
   pastry, thawed, or ½ quantity
   puff pastry (see page 148)

caster sugar, for dredging

150 ml (5 fl oz) double cream

75 ml (3 fl oz) single cream

1 Roll out the pastry on a lightly
   floured working surface to a
rectangle measuring 30 × 25 cm
(12 × 10 inches).

2 Dredge with caster sugar. Fold
   the long sides of the puff pastry
halfway towards the centre.

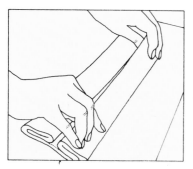

3 Dredge with more caster sugar
   and fold again, taking the sides
right to the centre.

4 Dredge with sugar again and
   fold in half lengthways, hiding
the first folds and pressing lightly.

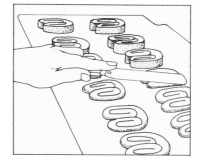

5 Cut across the pastry length
   into 24 equal-sized slices.
Dampen a baking sheet and place
the palmiers on it, cut-side down.
Flatten them slightly with a palette
knife or the palm of your hand.

6 Bake in the oven at 220°C
   (425°F) mark 7 for 8 minutes
until golden brown. Turn each
over and bake for a further 4
minutes. Transfer to a wire rack
and leave for about 20 minutes to
cool.

7 Whip the creams together with
   a little caster sugar, until lightly
peaked. Sandwich the palmiers
together with the cream before
serving. Sprinkle with caster sugar.

CREAM HORNS

| 1.45 | £ | ✳* | 247 cals |

*after stage 4

Makes 8

212-g (7½-oz) packet frozen puff
  pastry, thawed, or ¼ quantity
  puff pastry (see page 148)

beaten egg, to glaze

raspberry jam

150 ml (5 fl oz) double cream

75 ml (3 fl oz) single cream

icing sugar, to decorate

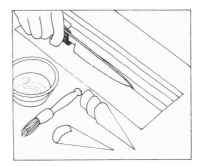

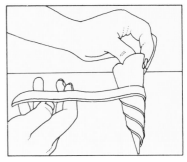

1 Roll out the pastry on a lightly
floured working surface to a
strip measuring 66 × 10 cm (26 × 4
inches). Cut the pastry lengthways
with a sharp knife into eight 1-cm
(½-inch) ribbons.

2 Grease eight cream horn tins.
Moisten one edge of each
pastry strip and wind each round a
horn tin starting at the tip, overlapping 3 mm (⅛ inch) and finishing neatly on underside. The
pastry should not overlap the
metal rim. Brush with beaten egg.

3 Dampen a baking sheet and
arrange the cream horns on it,
join-side down. Bake in the oven
at 220°C (425°F) mark 7 for 10
minutes until golden brown.

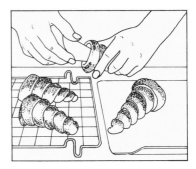

4 Cool for a few minutes then
carefully twist each tin, holding the pastry lightly in the other
hand, to ease it out of the pastry
horn. Leave the horns for about 30
minutes to cool completely.

5 When cold, fill the tip of each
horn with a little jam. Whip
the two creams together until stiff
and fill the horns down to the jam.
Sift the icing sugar and use to
dredge the horns.

CARAMEL BANANA TORTE

1.45* ☐ ☐ ✳* | 403 cals

* plus 2 hours cooling; freeze after
stage 4

Serves 8

175 g (6 oz) self-raising flour
1.25 ml ($\frac{1}{4}$ tsp) baking powder
1.25 ml ($\frac{1}{4}$ tsp) bicarbonate of soda
50 g (2 oz) butter, cut into pieces
150 g (5 oz) caster sugar
350 g (12 oz) ripe bananas
2.5 ml ($\frac{1}{2}$ tsp) freshly grated nutmeg
45 ml (3 tbsp) milk
1 egg, beaten
75 g (3 oz) sugar
175 g (6 oz) full fat soft cheese
30 ml (2 tbsp) lemon juice
30 ml (2 tbsp) icing sugar
50 g (2 oz) flaked almonds, browned

1 Grease a 20-cm (8-inch) round
cake tin. Base-line with greaseproof paper and grease the paper.

2 Sift the flour, baking powder
and bicarbonate of soda into a
bowl. Rub in the butter until the
mixture resembles fine breadcrumbs then stir in the caster sugar.

3 Peel half the bananas and mash
them in a bowl then beat in
the grated nutmeg, milk and egg
and stir into the dry ingredients.
Turn the mixture into the prepared tin and level the surface.

4 Bake in the oven at 180°C
(350°F) mark 4 for about 40
minutes or until a warmed fine
skewer inserted in the centre comes
out clean. Cool in tin for 5 minutes
before turning out on to wire rack
to cool completely (about 2 hours).
Slice the cake in half horizontally.

5 Make the caramel. Put rest of
sugar into a small pan. Dissolve,
without stirring, over gentle heat,
then boil until a rich brown colour.

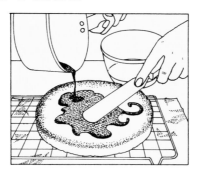

6 When the caramel is ready,
immediately pour it over the
top surface of the cake. Use an
oiled knife to spread the caramel
over the cake.

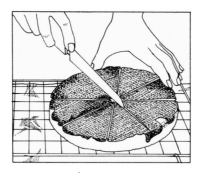

7 Mark the caramel topped cake
into eight portions with the
point of a knife.

8 Put the soft cheese, lemon juice
and icing sugar into a bowl
and beat together. Peel and chop
the remaining bananas and add to
half of the cheese mixture. Use to
sandwich the cakes together.

9 Spread a little cheese mixture
around the sides and cover with
most of the almonds. Decorate top
with the remaining cheese mixture
and almonds.

ECLAIRS

1.45* ⬚ £ ✳* 213 cals*

* includes 20–30 minutes cooling;
freeze after stage 3; 201 cals with
plain chocolate

Makes 12

1 quantity choux pastry (see page 149)

300 ml (10 fl oz) double cream

1 quantity chocolate glacé icing (see page 154) or 50 g (2 oz) plain chocolate

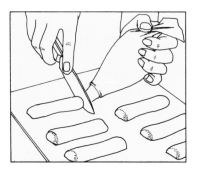

1 Dampen a baking sheet with water. Put the choux pastry into a piping bag fitted with a medium plain nozzle and pipe fingers, 9 cm (3½ inches) long, on to the baking sheet, keeping the lengths even and cutting the pastry off with a wet knife.

2 Bake in the oven at 200°C (400°F) mark 6 for about 35 minutes until crisp and golden.

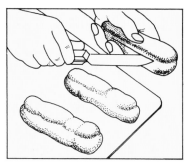

3 Make a slit down the side of each bun with a sharp, pointed knife to release the steam then transfer to a wire rack and leave for 20–30 minutes to cool completely.

4 Just before serving, whip the double cream until stiff and use it to fill the éclairs.

5 Ice with chocolate glacé icing or break the chocolate into a heatproof bowl and place over simmering water. Stir until the chocolate is melted.

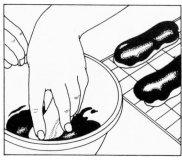

6 Pour into a shallow bowl and dip in the filled éclairs, drawing each one across the surface of the chocolate.

——— VARIATIONS ———

For less rich éclairs, replace the double cream with 300 ml (½ pint) crème pâtissière (see page 155). Although chocolate is the favourite flavour for éclairs, ring the changes with coffee glacé icing (see page 154).

To make savoury éclairs for a cocktail party, shape the choux pastry into very small éclairs and bake for 15–20 minutes. When cold, fill them with a mixture of 100 g (4 oz) full fat soft cheese creamed with 50 g (2 oz) butter and seasoned with 5 ml (1 tsp) lemon juice and salt and pepper to taste. Or cream 100 g (4 oz) full fat soft cheese with 50 g (2 oz) butter, 10 ml (2 tsp) tomato purée, a few drops of Worcestershire sauce and salt and pepper to taste. For anchovy éclairs, cream 175–225 g (6–8 oz) butter with 10 ml (2 tsp) anchovy essence and pepper to taste; pipe into the éclairs when cold.

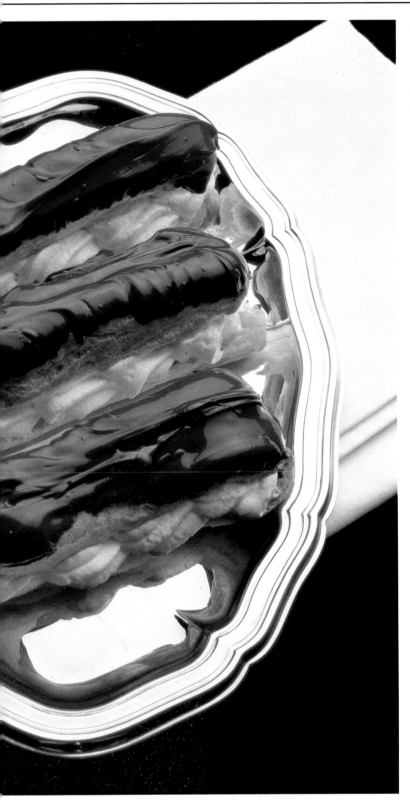

GLAZED FRUIT TARTS

Illustrated on front cover

| 2.00 | 🗍 £ £ ✳* | 377 cals |

* after stage 2

Makes 8

1 quantity pâte sucrée (see page 146)

150 ml (5 fl oz) double cream

50 ml (2 fl oz) single cream

225 g (8 oz) fresh strawberries

60 ml (4 tbsp) redcurrant jelly, to glaze

1 Roll out the pâte sucrée on a lightly floured working surface and use to line eight 9-cm (3½-inch) shallow patty tins.

2 Bake 'blind' in the oven at 190°C (375°F) mark 5 for 15–20 minutes until pale golden. Turn out on to a wire rack and leave for 30 minutes to cool.

3 Whip the double and single creams together until stiff. Spread a layer of cream over the tart bases.

4 Using a sharp knife, slice the strawberries. Arrange on top of the cream in an overlapping circle on each tart.

5 Melt the redcurrant jelly over a very low heat, adding a little water if necessary. Brush over the strawberries to glaze.

STRAWBERRY SAVARIN

2.00* ☐ £ £ ✳* 257 cals

* plus 1 hour chilling if served cold;
freeze after baking in stage 5

Serves 6

15 g (½ oz) fresh yeast or 7.5 ml
   (1½ tsp) dried yeast plus a pinch
   of sugar

45 ml (3 tbsp) tepid milk

2 eggs, lightly beaten

50 g (2 oz) butter, melted and
   cooled

100 g (4 oz) plain flour

15 ml (1 tbsp) caster sugar

25 g (1 oz) desiccated coconut

90 ml (6 tbsp) redcurrant jelly or
   sieved strawberry jam

75 ml (5 tbsp) lemon juice

225 g (8 oz) strawberries, hulled
   and thinly sliced

1 Lightly oil a 1.3-litre (2¼-pint)
savarin tin or ring mould and
turn it upside down on absorbent
kitchen paper to drain off the
excess oil.

2 Crumble the fresh yeast into a
bowl and cream with the tepid
milk until smooth. If using the
dried yeast and sugar, sprinkle the
mixture into the tepid milk and
leave in a warm place for 15
minutes until frothy. Gradually
beat the eggs and butter into the
yeast liquid.

3 Mix the flour in a bowl with
the sugar and coconut. With a
wooden spoon, gradually stir in
the yeast mixture to form a thick
smooth batter.

4 Turn into the prepared tin,
cover and leave to rise for about
30 minutes or until the savarin is
nearly doubled in size.

5 Bake in the oven at 190°C
(375°F) mark 5 for 35–40
minutes until golden. Turn out on
to a wire rack placed over a large
plate. Put the jelly and lemon
juice into a small pan over low
heat.

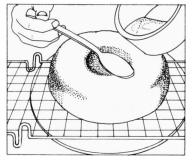

6 When the jelly is melted spoon
over the warm savarin until
well glazed, allowing any excess to
collect on the plate under the wire
rack. Transfer the savarin to a
serving plate.

7 Return the excess jelly mixture
to the pan and add the strawberries; stir to coat. Remove from
heat and cool for 15–20 minutes
or until almost set, then spoon
over the savarin. Serve warm or
cold with soured cream.

——— VARIATION ———

To make Strawberry babas, divide
the yeast batter between six 9-cm
(3½-inch) ring tins. Leave to rise
until the moulds are nearly two-
thirds full then bake for 15–20
minutes. Replace the lemon juice
with brandy or kirsch, soak each
baba well and place on individual
serving plates. Finish with strawberries and soured cream as above.

GÂTEAU ST HONORÉ

| 2.00 | 🍴🍴🍴 £ £ ✳* | 709 cals |

* after stage 5

Serves 6

1 quantity pâte sucrée (page 146)

beaten egg, to glaze

1 quantity choux pastry (page 149)

300 ml (10 fl oz) double cream

45 ml (3 tbsp) sugar

45 ml (3 tbsp) water

1 quantity crème pâtissière
(page 155)

angelica and glacé cherries

1 Roll out the pâte sucrée on a
lightly floured working surface
to an 18-cm (7-inch) round. Place
on a baking sheet and prick all
over with a fork. Brush a 1 cm
(½ inch) band round the edge with
beaten egg.

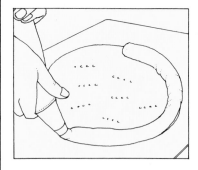

2 Put the choux pastry into a
piping bag fitted with a medium
plain nozzle and pipe a circle round
the edge. Brush with beaten egg.

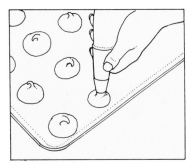

3 Dampen a baking sheet and
pipe about twenty walnut-sized
choux balls on to it. Brush with
beaten egg.

4 Bake both the flan and the
choux balls in the oven at 190°C
(375°F) mark 5 for about 15
minutes or until well risen and
golden brown.

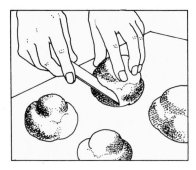

5 Make a slit in the side of each
bun to release the steam, then
transfer with the flan on to a wire
rack and leave for 15–20 minutes
to cool.

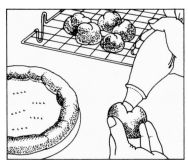

6 Whip the cream until stiff. Reserving a little cream for the
top of the gateau, put the rest into
a piping bag fitted with a medium
plain nozzle and pipe some into
each of the cold choux buns.

7 Put the sugar with the water
into a heavy based saucepan
and boil until the edge just begins
to turn straw-coloured. Dip the
tops of the choux buns in this
syrup, using a skewer or tongs to
hold them.

8 Use the remainder of the syrup
to stick the buns on to the
choux pastry border to form a wall.
Fill the centre of the gateau with
the crème pâtissière mixture.

9 Pipe the reserved cream
around the edge, in between
the choux balls. Decorate with
angelica and cherries.

ST HONORÉ

This Parisian speciality is named
in honour of an early French
bishop, honoured as the patron
saint of bakers and *pâtissiers*.
Gâteau St Honoré is a classic,
always made with two types of
pastry and two types of cream,
assembled with the rich golden
glaze of caramel. Pâte sucrée is
used for the base, an ideal lining
pastry to hold the crème pâtissière
filling. The piped choux pastry
that forms the walls of the gâteau
is crisp and golden outside,
hollow inside to take generous
quantities of whipped double
cream. Complete the decoration
if you wish with spun sugar (see
page 84).

LEMON AND PASSION-FRUIT GÂTEAU

1.30* £ £ ✻*	278–347 cals

* plus 1–2 hours cooling and 2–3 hours macerating; freeze after stage 5

Serves 8–10

50 g (2 oz) butter

4 eggs

125 g (4 oz) caster sugar

finely grated rind and juice of 1 lemon

125 g (4 oz) plain flour

225 g (8 oz) strawberries, hulled and thinly sliced

50 g (2 oz) icing sugar

3 passion-fruit

150 ml (5 fl oz) whipping cream

142 ml (5 fl oz) soured cream

1 Grease a deep 20-cm (8-inch) round cake tin. Base-line with greaseproof paper. Grease paper, then dust with sugar and flour.

2 Melt the butter in a small saucepan; do not boil. Remove from the heat and cool for 10 minutes.

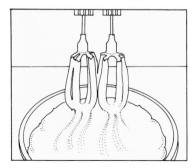

3 In another bowl, whisk together the eggs, caster sugar and lemon rind until very pale and thick enough to leave a trail. Sift the flour over the egg mixture.

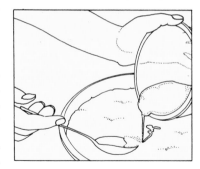

4 Drizzle over the butter. Fold in thoroughly. Turn the mixture into the prepared tin.

5 Bake in the oven at 190°C (375°F) mark 5 for 35–40 minutes or until a fine warmed skewer inserted in the centre comes out clean. Turn out on to a wire rack and cool for 1–2 hours.

6 Meanwhile, put the strawberries into a bowl with the lemon juice and 25 g (1 oz) icing sugar and leave to macerate for 2–3 hours. When the cake is cold, split in half and drizzle both halves with the juices from the fruit.

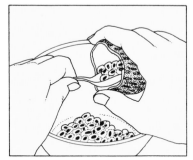

7 Using a sharp knife, cut the passion-fruit in half and scoop out the pulp. Discard the skin. Lightly whip the cream, fold in the soured cream and passion-fruit seeds.

8 Sandwich the cakes together with the strawberries and cream mixture and dust with the remaining icing sugar to serve.

WALNUT MERINGUE CAKE

3.00* £ ✳	528 cals

* plus 1 hour cooling and 2 hours chilling

Serves 6

4 egg whites

175 g (6 oz) caster sugar

2.5 ml (½ tsp) white wine vinegar

75 g (3 oz) walnut pieces, chopped

300 ml (10 fl oz) double cream

200 ml (7 fl oz) lemon curd

chocolate curls, to decorate

1 Line two baking sheets with non-stick paper. Whisk the egg whites to stiff peaks.

2 Beat in 30 ml (2 tbsp) sugar with the vinegar. Fold in the walnuts with the remaining sugar.

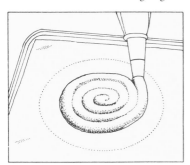

3 Spoon the meringue mixture into a piping bag fitted with a 1-cm (½-inch) plain nozzle. Pipe out two 20-cm (8-inch) rounds on the prepared baking sheets.

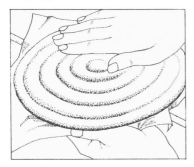

4 Bake in the oven at 110°C (225°F) mark ¼ for about 2 hours. Ease off the paper and place on wire racks for 1 hour to cool.

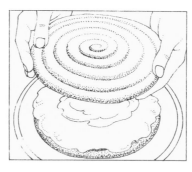

5 Whip cream until it holds its shape. Place one meringue on a dish; top with half cream.

6 Spoon the lemon curd into the centre of the cream and top with the second meringue round. Pipe the remaining cream around the edge. Refrigerate for 2 hours, then decorate with chocolate curls.

— VARIATION —

For a change, you can always use chopped hazel nuts or chopped almonds. Instead of chocolate curls, finely chopped nuts or praline are good alternatives.

FROZEN RASPBERRY MERINGUE

| 0.30* | £ £ | ✳* | 454 cals |

* plus at least 3 hours cooling and 6
hours freezing; freeze after stage 4

Serves 6

700 g (1½ lb) fresh raspberries,
   hulled

60 ml (4 tbsp) icing sugar

60 ml (4 tbsp) orange-flavoured
   liqueur

300 ml (10 fl oz) double cream

150 ml (5 fl oz) single cream

18 meringue shells (made from
   3 egg whites, see page 140)

1 Put half the raspberries into a large bowl. Sift over the icing sugar, add the liqueur and mix gently. Cover and leave in a cool place for 3–4 hours or overnight until the raspberry juices run.

2 Purée the raspberry mixture in a blender or food processor until smooth and press through a nylon sieve to remove the pips.

3 Whip the creams together until they just hold their shape. Break up the meringues into 3–4 pieces each and stir through the cream with the raspberry purée until just mixed but still marbled in appearance.

4 Oil a 1.7-litre (3-pint) ring mould. Spoon the mixture into the prepared mould, overwrap and freeze at least 6 hours.

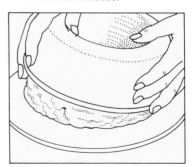

5 To serve: take straight from the freezer. Ease out of the mould and pile the remaining raspberries in the centre.

RASPBERRY ROULADE

1.00* 🔲 £ £ ✳* 448 cals

* plus 30 minutes cooling; freeze after rolling the roulade

Serves 6

450 g (1 lb) raspberries, hulled

5 eggs, separated

125 g (4 oz) caster sugar

50 g (2 oz) plain flour

30 ml (2 tbsp) orange-flavoured liqueur

300 ml (10 fl oz) double cream

45 ml (3 tbsp) icing sugar

1 Cut out two sheets of grease-proof paper and one of foil, 38 × 40 cm (15 × 16 inches) each.

2 Place the papers on top of each other with the foil underneath. Fold up 4 cm (1½ inches) on all four sides and secure the corners with paperclips to form a case.

3 Brush the case out with melted lard, and when set, dust with caster sugar. Put the case on a baking sheet.

4 Put half the raspberries into a blender and work until just smooth, then press through a nylon sieve to remove the pips.

5 Whisk the egg yolks in a deep bowl with the caster sugar until really thick. Gradually whisk in the raspberry purée, keeping the mixture stiff.

6 Sift the flour over the surface and fold lightly into the egg and raspberry mixture.

7 Whisk the egg whites until stiff, and fold them gently through the raspberry mixture.

8 Turn into the prepared paper case and smooth the surface. Bake in the oven at 200°C (400°F) mark 6 for about 12 minutes or until the mixture springs back when pressed lightly with a finger.

9 Cover immediately with a sheet of greaseproof paper which has been wrung out under the cold tap. Lay a clean tea towel over the top and leave for about 30 minutes to cool.

10 Meanwhile, reserving six raspberries for decoration, sprinkle the rest with the liqueur and sift over the icing sugar. Whip the cream until it is just stiff enough to hold its shape.

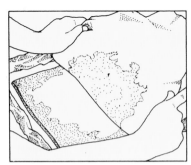

11 Remove the cloth from the roulade and carefully ease off the top greaseproof paper. Remove the paperclips. Trim the edges of the roulade, spread three quarters of the cream over the top and scatter with raspberries.

12 Carefully roll up the roulade, gradually easing off the paper. Roll on to a large flat serving plate and decorate with whirls of cream. Just before serving, dust with sieved icing sugar and decorate with the reserved raspberries.

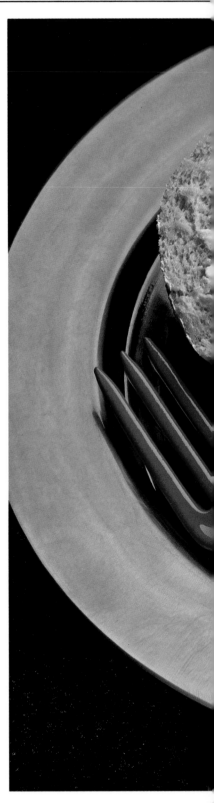

APFEL STRUDEL

2.45* 🔲 🔲 £	321–401 cals

* plus 1 hour standing time

Serves 8–10

225 g (8 oz) plain flour
2.5 ml (½ tsp) salt
1 egg, slightly beaten
30 ml (2 tbsp) vegetable oil
60 ml (4 tbsp) lukewarm water
45 ml (3 tbsp) seedless raisins
45 ml (3 tbsp) currants
75 g (3 oz) caster sugar
2.5 ml (½ tsp) ground cinnamon
1 kg (2¼ lb) cooking apples, peeled, cored and grated
45 ml (3 tbsp) melted butter
100 g (4 oz) ground almonds
icing sugar, to decorate

1 Lightly oil a baking sheet. Put the flour and salt into a large bowl, make a well in the centre and pour in the egg and oil.

2 Add the water gradually, stirring with a fork to make a soft, sticky dough. Work the dough in the bowl until it leaves the sides, then turn it out on to a lightly floured surface and knead for about 15 minutes.

3 Form into a ball, place on a cloth and cover with a warmed bowl. Leave to 'rest' in a warm place for 1 hour. Put the raisins, currants, sugar, cinnamon and apples into a bowl and mix together thoroughly.

4 Warm the rolling pin. Spread a clean cotton cloth on the table and sprinkle lightly with 15–30 ml (1–2 tbsp) flour.

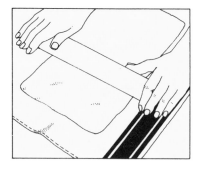

5 Place the dough on the cloth and roll out into a rectangle about 3 mm (⅛ inch) thick, lifting and turning it to prevent sticking.

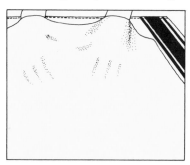

6 Gently stretch the dough, working from the centre to the outside, until it is paper-thin.

7 Trim the edges to form a rectangle about 68.5 × 61 cm (27 × 24 inches). Leave the strudel dough on the cloth to dry and 'rest' for 15 minutes.

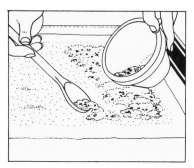

8 Position the dough with one of the long sides towards you, brush with melted butter and sprinkle with ground almonds.

9 Spread the apple mixture over the dough, leaving a 5-cm (2-inch) border uncovered all round the edge. Fold these pastry edges over the apple mixture, towards the centre.

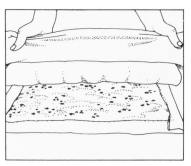

10 Lift the corners of the cloth nearest to you over the pastry, and roll up the strudel. Stop after each turn to pat into shape and to keep the roll even.

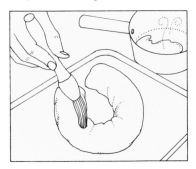

11 Form the roll into a horseshoe shape, slide it on to the prepared baking sheet and brush it with melted butter.

12 Bake in the oven at 190°C (375°F) mark 5 for about 40 minutes or until golden brown. Dredge the strudel with icing sugar. Serve hot or cold, in slices, with cream.

STRAWBERRY SHORTCAKES

| 1.30 | £ £ ✳* | 611 cals |

* after stage 6

Serves 6

| 275 g (10 oz) self-raising flour |
| 7.5 ml (1½ tsp) baking powder |
| good pinch of salt |
| 75 g (3 oz) butter, cut into nut-size pieces |
| 50 g (2 oz) caster sugar |
| 1 egg, beaten |
| few drops vanilla flavouring |
| 75–90 ml (5–6 tbsp) milk |
| 450 g (1 lb) fresh strawberries, 6 set aside, the remainder hulled |
| 30 ml (2 tbsp) orange-flavoured liqueur |
| 30 ml (2 tbsp) icing sugar |
| 300 ml (10 fl oz) double or whipping cream |
| 45 ml (3 tbsp) redcurrant jelly |

1 Brush a little melted lard over a large flat baking sheet; leave to cool for about 5 minutes. Dust the surface lightly with flour.

2 Sift the flour, baking powder and salt into a bowl. Rub in the butter until the mixture resembles breadcrumbs. Stir in the caster sugar.

3 Make a well in the centre of the dry ingredients and add the egg, vanilla flavouring and milk. Using a palette knife, cut through the dry ingredients until evenly blended, then quickly and lightly bring the mixture together using the fingertips of one hand.

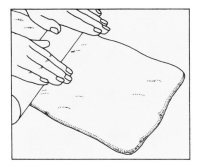

4 Turn the dough out on to a lightly floured surface and knead gently until just smooth. Roll out to a thickness of 1 cm (½ inch) and cut out six 9-cm (3½-inch) fluted rounds.

5 Gather up the scraps, knead lightly and roll out again. Place on the prepared baking sheet.

6 Brush the tops of the rounds with milk—don't let it trickle down the sides. Bake in the oven at 230°C (450°F) mark 8 for about 11 minutes or until the shortcakes are well risen and golden brown. Remove from the oven and keep warm.

7 Thickly slice half the strawberries. Put into a bowl and add the liqueur. Sieve in half the icing sugar.

8 With a fork, lightly crush the remaining strawberries and sieve in the rest of the icing sugar. Whip the cream until it just holds its shape and stir in the crushed strawberries.

9 Cut the shortcakes in half while they are still warm. Carefully run the point of a sharp knife from the side of the shortcake into the centre.

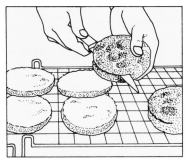

10 Rotate the shortcake and saw with the sharp knife until the cake is cut in two.

11 Spoon half the cream on to the shortcake bases and cover with the sliced strawberries. Spoon over the remaining cream and replace the shortcake tops.

12 Put the redcurrant jelly into a small pan and heat gently until liquid. Cool for 5–10 minutes, then brush over the shortcakes. Decorate with whole strawberries.

——————— VARIATION ———————

Any other soft fruits such as raspberries, loganberries, black-berries, bilberries or redcurrants can be used as an alternative filling for these delicious shortcakes. Skinned and roughly chopped peaches and nectarines would also be delicious. The tart flavour of berries or currants can be counter-acted by adding a little more sugar.

FRESH APRICOT FLAN

1.30* 🍮 £ £ ✳ 384 cals

* plus 2 hours chilling

Serves 6

150 g (5 oz) plain flour

50 g (2 oz) ground almonds

75 g (3 oz) butter or block margarine, cut into pieces

1 egg yolk mixed with 15 ml (1 tbsp) water

2 eggs

150 ml (5 fl oz) single cream

15 ml (1 tbsp) caster sugar

few drops almond flavouring

120 ml (8 tbsp) apricot jam, sieved

450 g (1 lb) fresh apricots, skinned, halved and stoned or one 411-g (14-oz) can apricot halves, drained

15 ml (1 tbsp) lemon juice

15 ml (1 tbsp) almond-flavoured liqueur

1 Mix the flour in a bowl with half the ground almonds. Rub in the butter until the mixture resembles fine breadcrumbs. Bind to a firm dough with the egg yolk mixture; knead lightly until smooth.

2 Roll out the dough on a lightly floured working surface and use to line a 22-cm (8½-inch) loose-bottomed French fluted flan tin. Bake 'blind' in the oven at 190°C (375°F) mark 5 for 15–20 minutes until set but not browned.

3 Meanwhile, mix the eggs, cream, sugar, remaining ground almonds and almond flavouring.

4 Warm the jam gently in a small saucepan. When the flan is set, spread 45 ml (3 tbsp) jam over base. Pour cream mixture into flan.

5 Increase the oven to 170°C (325°F) mark 3; return flan to it for 20 minutes or until the filling is just set; leave for about 1 hour to cool.

7 Add the lemon juice to the remaining jam together with the liqueur and reduce the mixture to a glaze. Brush over the apricots to cover them completely. Refrigerate for 2 hours before serving.

6 Arrange the apricot halves neatly over the custard filling in the flan.

CARROT CAKE

2.30* £ ✳* 616 cals

* begin a day ahead; allow 2 hours cooling; freeze after stage 6

Serves 8

225 g (8 oz) butter

225 g (8 oz) caster sugar

4 eggs, beaten

225 g (8 oz) self-raising flour

grated rind and juice of 1 large lemon

225 g (8 oz) carrots, peeled and finely grated

100 g (4 oz) ground almonds or finely chopped walnuts

15 ml (1 tbsp) kirsch (optional)

75 g (3 oz) full fat soft cheese

50 g (2 oz) icing sugar

shredded orange rind, to decorate

1 Grease a 20-cm (8-inch) round cake tin. Line with greaseproof paper and grease the paper.

2 Put the butter and sugar into a bowl and beat together until pale and fluffy. Add the eggs, a little at a time, beating well after each addition.

3 Fold in the flour with the lemon rind and juice, reserving 5 ml (1 tsp) juice.

4 Stir in the carrots, almonds and kirsch, if using. Spoon the mixture into the prepared tin and level the surface.

5 Bake in the oven at 180°C (350°F) mark 4 for 1½ hours until well risen and golden brown or until a fine warmed skewer inserted in the centre comes out clean. Check after 1¼ hours. Cover with foil if overbrowning.

6 Turn out on to a wire rack and leave to cool for about 2 hours. Preferably keep the cake until the following day before icing and serving.

7 Make the icing. Put the cheese, reserved lemon juice and the icing sugar into a bowl and beat until soft and creamy.

8 Spread over the top of the cake using a palette knife to swirl the icing. Decorate with shredded orange rind.

DOBOS TORTE

| 2.10 | 🗍 🗍 £ | 655 cals |

Serves 8

4 eggs

275 g (10 oz) caster sugar

150 g (5 oz) plain flour

100 g (4 oz) plain chocolate

3 egg whites

175 g (6 oz) icing sugar

225 g (8 oz) butter

50 g (2 oz) crushed biscuits or
  chopped nuts, to decorate

1 Line two baking sheets with non-stick paper. Put the whole eggs into a heatproof bowl with 175 g (6 oz) caster sugar and place over simmering water, whisking until the mixture is thick enough to leave a trail on the surface when the whisk is lifted, then remove from the heat.

2 Sift half the flour over the mixture and fold in lightly with a metal spoon. Add the remaining flour in the same way.

3 Carefully spread some of the mixture out on the baking sheets in large rounds measuring about 20 cm (8 inches) in diameter. Bake in the oven at 190°C (375°F) mark 5 for 7–10 minutes until golden brown.

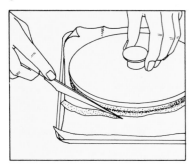

4 Loosen from the baking sheets and trim each round to a neat shape with a sharp knife, using a saucepan lid as a guide. Transfer them on to wire racks and leave for about 15 minutes to cool.

5 Re-line the baking sheets, spread on more mixture. Bake, trim and cool as before. There will be enough mixture to make six or seven rounds.

6 Select the round with the best surface and lay it on an oiled baking sheet.

7 Put the remaining caster sugar in a small, heavy based saucepan. Over a gentle heat, dissolve the sugar, without stirring, and boil it steadily to a rich brown.

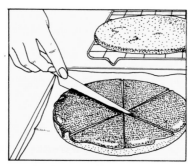

8 Pour it over the round on the baking sheet, spreading it with a knife brushed with oil. Mark into eight sections and trim round the edge.

9 Break the chocolate into a heatproof bowl and place over simmering water. Stir until the chocolate is melted, then remove from the heat.

10 Put the egg whites and icing sugar into a heatproof bowl and place over simmering water. Whisk until very thick, then remove from the heat.

11 Put the butter into a bowl and beat until pale and soft. Beat the egg and sugar mixture into it gradually, then stir in the melted chocolate.

12 Sandwich the remaining biscuit rounds together with some of the filling and put the caramel-covered one on top.

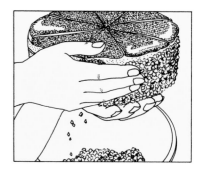

13 Spread the sides of the torte with more filling and press the crushed biscuit crumbs or chopped nuts round the sides.

14 Spoon the remaining filling into a piping bag fitted with a star nozzle and pipe a decorative border round the top edge.

––––––––– VARIATION –––––––––

For a simpler filling, melt 50 g (2 oz) plain chocolate as above and leave to cool slightly. Cream 150 g (5 oz) butter and gradually beat in 225 g (8 oz) sifted icing sugar. Beat in the melted chocolate while it is still soft.

DOBOS TORTE

The old Austro-Hungarian empire is the home of this elaborate 'drum cake'. Versions of the traditional sponge rounds, layered with chocolate cream and glazed with caramel, are still to be found in the best cafés and pastry shops from Vienna to Budapest.

Be sure to mark the caramel into portions before it hardens or it will be extremely difficult to cut.

DANISH PASTRIES

| 2.15 | ⬠ ⬠ £ ✳* | 451 cals |

* freeze before icing in stage 14

Makes 16

175 g (6 oz) lard, softened
240 g (8½ oz) butter, softened
450 g (1 lb) plain flour
5 ml (1 tsp) salt
140 g (5½ oz) caster sugar
25 g (1 oz) fresh yeast or 15 ml
   (1 tbsp) dried yeast plus a pinch
   of sugar
about 200 ml (7 fl oz) tepid milk
2 eggs, beaten
40 g (1½ oz) ground almonds
2.5 ml (½ tsp) almond flavouring
10 ml (2 tsp) ground cinnamon
glacé icing (see page 154)
25 g (1 oz) sultanas
4–6 glacé cherries

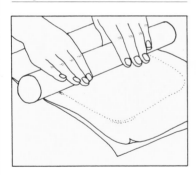

1 Place a sheet of greaseproof paper on a work surface. Lay 150 g (5 oz) lard on it and 175 g (6 oz) butter on top of the lard. Cover with greaseproof paper. Roll out to a 23-cm (9-inch) square.

2 Ease off the top sheet of paper and, using a palette knife, square the edges of the fat.

3 Sift the flour and salt into a bowl and rub in the remaining lard, stir in 50 g (2 oz) caster sugar.

4 Crumble the yeast into a bowl and cream with the milk until smooth. If using the dried yeast and sugar, sprinkle the mixture into the milk and leave in a warm place for 15 minutes until frothy.

5 Add the yeast liquid to the dry ingredients with half the beaten egg. Mix to a soft dough, adding more milk if necessary. Knead well until smooth, about 10 minutes.

6 Roll out on a floured surface to a 28–30 cm (11–12 inch) square.

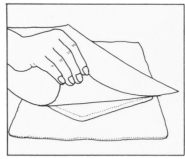

7 Place the square of fat on top of the dough, at right angles.

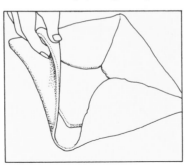

8 Fold each triangular corner of dough over the fat to form an envelope. Press the joins to seal.

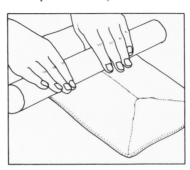

9 Turn dough squarely in front of you. Roll the dough out gently to an oblong.

10 Fold the top third down and the bottom third up, brush off excess flour. Turn the dough through 90° and repeat rolling and folding. Place on a floured plate, cover with floured cling film and refrigerate for 15 minutes.

11 Make the almond paste. Put 15 g (½ oz) softened butter, 40 g (1½ oz) caster sugar, the ground almonds and the almond flavouring into a small bowl and beat together to give a firm paste.

12 Make the butter filling. Put the remaining butter and caster sugar into a bowl with the ground cinnamon and beat together until fluffy. Roll the dough into the required shapes (see page 128). (For each shape you will have to start by rolling one quarter of the dough out thinly.)

13 Cover all four baking sheets loosely with oiled cling film and leave to rise in a warm place for about 20 minutes, or until doubled in size. Glaze with beaten egg and bake at 220°C (425°F) mark 7 for about 10 minutes or until golden brown and crisp.

14 Ease the pastries off on to wire racks and, while warm, brush with a little glacé icing.

QUANTITIES

For the given amount of filling and pastry in this recipe, choose to make two almond-filled shapes and two cinnamon-filled shapes. This will then give 16 pastries comprising four different shapes.

DANISH PASTRY SHAPES

CUSHIONS AND FOLDOVERS

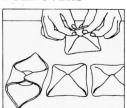

Cut into four 7.5-cm (3-inch) squares. Put a little almond paste in the centre. Fold over two opposite corners to the centre. Make a cushion by folding over all four corners, securing tips with beaten egg. Place on a baking sheet. To finish, see page 126, stage 14.

CRESCENTS

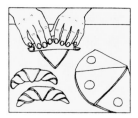

Cut out one 23-cm (9-inch) round. Divide into four segments and put a little almond paste at base of each.

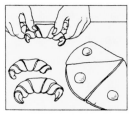

Roll up from base and curl round. Place on a baking sheet. To finish, see page 126, stage 14.

TWISTS

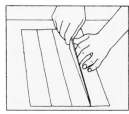

Cut into an oblong 30 × 20.5 cm (12 × 8 inches). Cut lengthways to give four pieces.

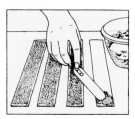

Spread half the cinnamon butter over the dough.

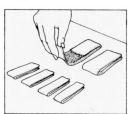

Fold bottom third of each up and the top third down, seal and cut each across into thin slices.

Twist these slices and put on a baking sheet. To finish, see page 126, stage 14.

IMPERIAL STARS

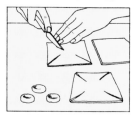

Cut into four 7.5-cm (3-inch) squares. Make diagonal cuts from each corner to within 1 cm (½ inch) of centre.

Put a piece of almond paste in centre of square and fold one corner of each cut section down to centre, securing tips with beaten egg. Place on a baking sheet. To finish, see page 126, stage 14.

PINWHEELS

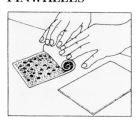

Cut into an oblong 30 × 20.5 cm (12 × 8 inches). Spread half the cinnamon butter over the oblong and sprinkle with the sultanas; roll up like a Swiss roll.

Cut into four 2.5-cm (1-inch) slices and place, cut-side upwards, on a backing sheet. To finish, see page 126, stage 14.

COCKSCOMBS

Cut into a square. Cut in turn into four equal squares. Spread a little almond paste over half of each square to within 1 cm (½ inch) of the edges.

Fold the squares in half and slit the folded edge with a knife in four places. Curve pastry to open into a comb shape, put on a baking sheet. To finish, see page 126, stage 14.

USEFUL INFORMATION
AND
BASIC RECIPES

Ingredients and Equipment

Cake making can never be a hit and miss affair—there are a few golden rules to success: read your recipe before you start, select and measure ingredients carefully, make sure your oven temperature is accurate and baking time is followed according to the recipe. Most cakes need to go into the oven as soon as they are mixed, so turn on the oven before you start mixing.

BASIC INGREDIENTS

FLOUR

Most cakes are made with plain or self-raising flour. Self-raising flour is popular for plain mixtures because it contains raising agents already blended into it. It contains too much raising agent for many rich cakes, however, so for these use either a mixture of self-raising and plain flours, or plain flour with the exact amount of raising agent specified. If a recipe calls for self-raising flour and you have none, use plain flour with baking powder added 12.5 ml (2½ tsp) to each 225 g (8 oz).

For cakes made with yeast, and puff pastries, use *strong plain flour* (sometimes called bread flour). This gives a large volume and light, open texture.

Wholemeal and *wheatmeal* flours can be used for variety of texture and flavour except in very light, delicate mixtures. When using these flours, add extra liquid to the recipe to give the right consistency.

Sift flours before using to incorporate air and make them easier to mix in.

FATS

Butter and *block margarine* are interchangeable, although butter gives a richer flavour and cakes made with butter keep well. *Soft tub margarines* are *only* suitable for special all-in-one recipes. Vegetable oil can be used in specially proportioned recipes.

Do not use butter and block margarine direct from the refrigerator. If the fat for a creamed mixture is too firm, beat it alone until softened, then add the sugar and cream them together. If melted fat is required, heat it very gently as it quickly turns brown.

SUGARS

Sugar is not just a sweetener; it also helps produce a soft, spongy texture and improves the keeping qualities of a cake.

Caster sugar is the best white sugar for most cakes as it dissolves quickly and easily.

Demerara sugar has coarse crystals that make it unsuitable for creamed mixtures. It is fine for cakes made by the melting method, (see page 141). It gives a golden colour and distinctive syrup flavour.

Granulated sugar is coarser than caster and less suitable for many cake recipes, although it is acceptable for rubbed-in mixtures. If used in creamed mixtures it produces a slightly reduced volume and a speckled crust.

Icing sugar is very fine and powdery, giving a poor volume and hard crust if used in cake mixtures. It is, however, ideal for icing and decorating.

Soft brown sugar creams well and, when used in place of caster sugar, gives an equally good volume. It gives a rich flavour and colour.

RAISING AGENTS

Baking powder reacts with moisture to produce carbon dioxide. The bubbles of gas expand during baking, making the cake rise. The heat then sets the mixture so that the bubbles are trapped.

One part bicarbonate of soda to two parts cream of tartar is sometimes used as a substitute.

Yeast is a living organism that ferments in a warm moist atmosphere to produce carbon dioxide. The yeast is then killed in the hot oven and the bubbles remain trapped in the structure of the flour. Many recipes are written using *fresh yeast*, but *dried yeast* works equally well if reconstituted in liquid before use.

Where a recipe states 25 g (1 oz) fresh yeast, use 15 ml (1 tbsp) dried yeast and follow the manufacturer's instructions.

Eggs used for baking should be at room temperature. A size 4 egg is suitable for most recipes.

MEASURING INGREDIENTS

When making cakes it is important to weigh and measure quantities accurately to achieve the correct balance of ingredients. Both metric and imperial measures are given in the recipes. Use one set only—metric figures are adjusted conversions and not exact equivalents.

Use scales for quantities of dry ingredients over 25 g (1 oz), spoon measures for smaller quantities. Use standard measuring spoons, available in sets of 2.5 ml, 5 ml, 10 ml and 15 ml (or $\frac{1}{4}$ tsp, $\frac{1}{2}$ tsp, 1 tsp and 1 tbsp). For dry ingredients dip the spoon in and level the surface with a knife. Liquids of course level themselves. For larger quantities of liquid use a measuring jug marked either in millilitres or fluid ounces. Always measure liquid at eye level; looking down on to the markings gives a distorted view and an inaccurate measure.

CAKE TINS

Choose good-quality, strong cake tins in a variety of shapes and sizes. Non-stick surfaces clean most easily and are particularly useful in small, awkwardly shaped tins. Some cake tins have a loose bottom or a loosening device to make it easier to remove the cake.

Use the size of tin specified in the recipe. Using too large a tin will tend to give a pale, flat and shrunken-looking cake; cakes baked in too small a tin will bulge over and lose their contours. If you do not have the tin specified, choose a slightly larger one. The mixture will be shallower and will take less time to cook, so test for doneness 5–10 minutes early.

If using a tin of a different shape from the one in the recipe, choose one with the same liquid capacity (test by filling right to the brim with water).

Flan rings and tins come in many forms. Round tins with plain or fluted sides and removable bases are primarily for pastry flan cases. For sponge flans, use a special flan tin with a raised base.

Loaf tins are used for cakes as well as bread. Two sizes are available: 450 g (1 lb) and 900 g (2 lb). A Balmoral is a fluted, concertina-shaped loaf tin.

Sandwich tins are shallow round tins with straight sides for making sandwich and layer cakes, in sizes 18–25.5 cm (7–10 inches). A moule à manqué tin is a deep sandwich tin with sloping sides.

Small cake tins and moulds come in sheets of 6, 9 or 12, or individually. There are shapes for buns, éclairs, sponge fingers etc.

Spring-release tins come complete with different loose bottoms.

Standard cake tins For everyday use, 15-cm (6-inch), 18-cm (7-inch) and 20.5-cm (8-inch) tins are adequate; for celebration cakes you may need larger sizes.

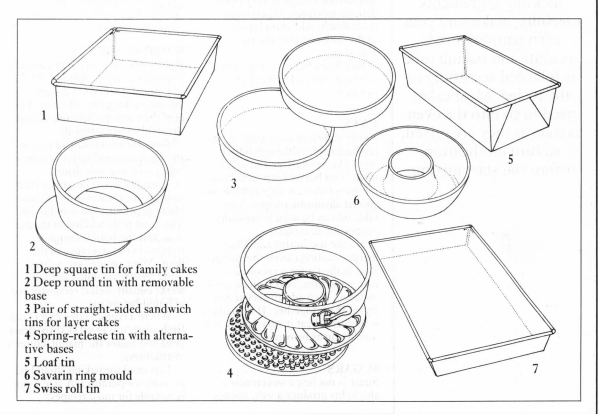

1 Deep square tin for family cakes
2 Deep round tin with removable base
3 Pair of straight-sided sandwich tins for layer cakes
4 Spring-release tin with alternative bases
5 Loaf tin
6 Savarin ring mould
7 Swiss roll tin

PREPARING CAKE TINS

Tins without a non-stick finish should be greased and lined before use. Non-stick tins do not need lining but may need greasing; follow the manufacturer's instructions. For a good finish to a sponge baked in a non-stick sandwich tin, grease the tin and then coat with a light mixture of sifted flour and caster sugar.

LINING TINS

Grease the tin by brushing with oil or melted fat and line it with greaseproof paper or non-stick (silicone treated) paper.

Lining a deep tin Cut a piece of greaseproof paper long enough to reach round the tin and wide enough to extend about 5 cm (2 inches) above the top. Cut another piece to fit the bottom. Fold up one edge of the long strip about 2.5 cm (1 inch), then snip the folded portion at intervals. Grease the tin, place the strip in position and then place the bottom piece over the snipped edge of the band to make a neat lining. Greaseproof paper should then be greased, non-stick paper does not require greasing.

Lining a sandwich tin Line the base only, cutting a round of greaseproof paper or non-stick paper to fit the base exactly.

TRICKS OF THE TRADE

- **Preheating the oven**
  Before starting to mix the cake, turn the oven to the correct setting so that it will be up to temperature by the time it is needed.

- **Testing whether a cake is cooked**
  Small cakes should be well risen, golden and just firm to the touch. They should start to shrink from the sides of the tin when taken out of the oven.

  A larger cake made with a light mixture should be spongy and give only very slightly when pressed in the centre with a finger; the surface should rise again immediately, leaving no impression.

  For a fruit cake, lift gently from the oven and listen to it. A sizzling sound indicates that the cake is not cooked through. Or insert a warmed fine skewer into the centre of the cake. It should come out perfectly clean.

- **Cooling the cake**
  Leave in the tin for a few minutes, then turn out gently and remove any lining paper. Turn the right way up on to a wire rack and leave until quite cold.

- **To skin hazelnuts**
  Heat through in the oven or under the grill, shaking them occasionally to turn. Then place in a clean cloth or polythene bag and rub the papery skins off.

- **To help prevent glacé cherries sinking**
  Cut cherries in half, rinse under cold running water, then pat dry and toss lightly in a little of the measured flour.

- **To shred or chop candied peel**
  Remove the sugar and cut the peel into fine shreds with scissors or chop with a sharp knife. If very hard, soak in boiling water for 1–2 minutes.

- **To blanch almonds**
  Put the nuts in a pan with cold water to cover, bring just to the boil, strain and run cold water over them. Rub between the finger and thumb to remove skins.

- **To toast nuts**
  Spread nuts in a shallow pan and brown lightly under a medium grill, turning occasionally; or bake in the oven at 180°C (350°F) mark 4 for 10–12 minutes.

- **To clean dried fruit**
  Most dried fruit is sold ready cleaned, washed and dried, if not, rub fruit on a wire sieve or in a tea towel with a little flour, then pick over to remove any stalks. Discard surplus flour. Stone raisins by working them between wet fingertips.

- **To separate an egg**
  Knock the egg sharply against the rim of a basin and break the shell in half. Pass the yolk back and forth from one half-shell to the other, letting the white drop into the basin. Put the yolk in another basin.

- **To melt chocolate**
  Break the chocolate into a bowl and stand it over hot (not boiling) water until melted. Do not allow to become too hot and only stir once or twice towards the end of melting.

- **To layer a cake**
  Measure the depth of the layers up the side of the cake and insert toothpicks at intervals as a cutting guide. Use a long, sharp-bladed knife, resting it above and against the toothpicks while cutting.

STORING AND FREEZING CAKES

When the cake is cold, store in a tin with just an airtight seal. Wrap fruit cakes in greaseproof paper and foil first. If no tin is available, store un-iced cakes wrapped first in greaseproof paper then in foil or cling film. Cakes with a fresh cream filling or decoration should be kept in the refrigerator. Store cakes and biscuits separately or biscuits will go soft.

Most undecorated cakes freeze well. Wrap plain cakes in freezer wrapping and seal before freezing.

Freeze decorated cakes without wrapping until firm, then wrap. Store in a rigid polythene container. Unwrap before thawing.

Freeze pastry cakes unfilled and refresh in the oven at 190°C (375°F) mark 5 for 5 minutes before filling and serving.

BASIC CAKE FREEZING KNOW-HOW

Storage time	Preparation	Freezing	Thawing and serving
CAKES *cooked* including sponge flans, Swiss rolls and layer cakes: 6 months *Iced cakes:* 2 months	Bake in usual way. Leave until cold on a wire rack. Swiss rolls are best rolled up in cornflour, not sugar, if they are to be frozen without a filling. Do not spread or layer cakes with jam before freezing. Keep essences to a minimum and go lightly on the spices.	Wrap plain cake layers separately, or together with waxed paper between layers. Open freeze iced cakes (whole or cut) until icing has set, then wrap. Seal and pack in boxes to protect the icing.	Iced cakes: unwrap before thawing, so the wrapping will not stick to the icing. Cream cakes: may be sliced while frozen for a better shape and quick thawing. Plain cakes: leave in package and thaw at room temperature. Un-iced large cakes thaw in about 3–4 hours at room temperature, layer cakes take about 1–2 hours and small cakes about 30 minutes: iced layer cakes take up to 4 hours.
CAKE MIXTURES *uncooked* 2 months	Whisked sponge mixtures do not freeze well uncooked. Put rich creamed mixtures into containers, or line the tin to be used later with greased foil and add the cake mixture.	Freeze uncovered. When frozen, remove from tin, package in foil and overwrap. Return to freezer.	To thaw, leave at room temperature for 2–3 hours, then fill tins to bake. Pre-formed cake mixtures can be returned to the original tin, without wrapping but still in foil lining. Place frozen in pre-heated oven and bake in usual way, but allow longer cooking time.
PASTRY* *uncooked* *Short pastries:* 3 months *Flaky pastries:* 3–4 months	Roll out to size required. Open freeze pie shells until hard, to avoid damage. Rounds of pastry can be stacked with wax paper between for pie bases or tops.	Stack pastry shapes with two pieces of waxed paper between layers: if needed, one piece of pastry can be removed without thawing the whole batch. Place the stack on a piece of cardboard, wrap and seal.	Thaw flat rounds at room temperature, fit into pie plate and proceed with recipe. Unbaked pie shells or flat cases should be returned to their original container before cooking: they can go into the oven from the freezer (ovenproof glass that has been in the freezer should first stand for 10 minutes at room temperature); add about 5 minutes to baking time.
PASTRY *cooked* *Pastry cases:* 6 months	Prepare as usual. Empty cases freeze satisfactorily, but with some change in texture.	Wrap carefully—very fragile.	Flan cases should be thawed at room temperature for about 1 hour. Refresh if wished, by heating, uncovered, in the oven at 170°C (325°F) mark 3 for 10 minutes.
CREAM *Whipped:* 3 months *Commercially frozen:* up to 1 year	Use only pasteurised cream, with a butterfat content of 40% or more (i.e. double cream). For best results, half-whip cream with 5 ml (1 tsp) caster sugar to each 150 ml (5 fl oz). Whipped cream may be piped into rosettes on waxed paper.	Transfer cream to suitable container, e.g. waxed carton, leaving head space for expansion. Open freeze rosettes; when firm, pack in a single layer in foil.	Thaw in refrigerator, allowing 24 hours, or 12 hours at room temperature. Put rosettes in position as decoration before thawing, as they cannot be handled once thawed. Rosettes take less time to thaw.

*Note there is little advantage in bulk-freezing uncooked shortcrust pastry, as it takes about 3 hours to thaw before it can be rolled out. For bulk-freezing flaky pastries—prepare up to the last rolling; pack in freezer bags or foil and overwrap. To use, leave for 3–4 hours at room temperature, or overnight in the refrigerator.

Cake-making Techniques

Plain or rich, fruity, spicy or laden with cream, cakes are pure fun. Wholly superfluous to our nutritional needs, they represent all that is sociable and pleasing about food. If you can master the techniques to produce a really beautiful cake you will give your family and friends a real treat—and yourself a lot of creative pleasure into the bargain.

RUBBED-IN CAKES

For plain cakes, in which the proportion of fat to flour is half or less, the fat is literally rubbed into the flour with the fingertips and thumbs. Cakes made like this have a soft, light texture, they are easy to make and economical too. Just because they are called 'plain' doesn't mean these cakes can't be varied with fruits and spices, but icings and fillings are generally kept to a minimum as these are the cakes that naturally form everyday tea-time fare for the family.

To make cakes by the 'rubbing in' method, first sift the dry ingredients into a bowl. Cut the firm fat into pieces and add to the bowl. Then rub the fat lightly into the flour between the fingertips and

thumbs. Lift your hands well up over the bowl and work lightly to incorporate air into the mixture; this helps to make the cake light, though the main raising agents are chemical. Shake the bowl occasionally to bring any large lumps to the surface and rub in until the mixture resembles fine breadcrumbs.

Sugar and flavourings go in next, then the liquid. Adding the liquid is a crucial stage in the making of a rubbed-in mixture. Too much liquid can cause a heavy, doughy texture, while insufficient gives a dry cake. Beaten egg and milk are the commonest liquids; add them cautiously, using just enough to bring the mixture to the right consistency. For cakes baked in a tin, the mixture should have a soft dropping consistency.

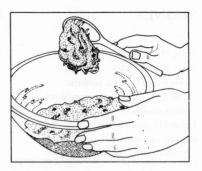

That is, it should drop easily from the spoon when the handle is tapped against the side of the bowl. For small cakes and buns that are baked flat on a baking sheet (such as rock buns or scones), the mixture should be stiff enough to hold

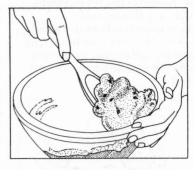

its shape without spreading too much during the baking time. A stiff consistency describes a mixture which clings to the spoon.

Because they are low in fat, these cakes do not keep well. They are best eaten the day they are made.

ALTERNATIVE RAISING AGENTS

If plain flour and baking powder are used instead of self-raising flour, allow 15 ml (1 tbsp) baking powder to 225 g (8 oz) flour and sift them together twice before using. If you use cream of tartar and bicarbonate of soda in place of baking powder, allow 5 ml (1 tsp) cream of tartar and 2.5 ml ($\frac{1}{2}$ tsp) bicarbonate of soda to 225 g (8 oz) plain flour with ordinary milk, or 2.5 ml ($\frac{1}{2}$ tsp) bicarbonate of soda and 2.5 ml ($\frac{1}{2}$ tsp) cream of tartar with soured milk.

SCONES

Makes 10–12

225 g (8 oz) self-raising flour
2.5 ml (½ tsp) salt
5 ml (1 tsp) baking powder
25–50 g (1–2 oz) butter or block
  margarine
150 ml (¼ pint) milk
beaten egg or milk, to glaze
  (optional)

1 Preheat a baking sheet in the oven. Sift together the flour, salt and baking powder into a bowl. Cut the butter into small pieces and add to the flour.

2 Rub in the fat until the mixture resembles fine breadcrumbs. Make a well in the centre and stir in enough milk to give a fairly soft dough. Turn it on to a floured working surface, and knead very lightly if necessary to remove any cracks.

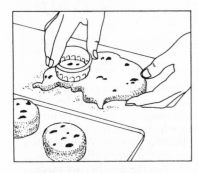

3 Roll out the dough lightly to about 2 cm (¾ inch) thick, or pat it out with the hand. Cut into rounds with a 5-cm (2-inch) cutter dipped in flour, or cut into triangles with a sharp knife.

4 Place on the baking sheet, brush if you wish with beaten egg or milk to glaze and bake in the hottest part of the oven at 230°C (450°F) mark 8 for 8–10 minutes until well risen and brown. Cool on a wire rack and serve split and buttered.

ROCK BUNS

Makes 12

225 g (8 oz) plain flour
pinch of salt
10 ml (2 tsp) baking powder
50 g (2 oz) butter or block
  margarine
50 g (2 oz) lard
75 g (3 oz) demerara sugar
75 g (3 oz) mixed dried fruit
grated rind of ½ a lemon
1 egg, beaten
a little milk

1 Lightly grease two baking sheets. Sift together the flour, salt and baking powder into a mixing bowl. Cut the butter and lard into small pieces and add it to the plain flour.

2 Rub the fat lightly into the flour between thumb and fingertips, holding the hands high above the bowl to keep the mixture cool and light. Shake the bowl occasionally to bring any large lumps to the surface. Rub in thoroughly until the mixture resembles fine breadcrumbs.

3 Add the sugar, fruit and lemon rind to the mixture and mix in thoroughly. Make a well in the centre, gradually pour in the beaten egg and mix with a fork. Add just enough milk to mix to a moist but stiff dough.

4 Using two forks, shape small quantities of mixture into rocky heaps on the prepared baking sheets.

5 Bake in the oven at 200°C (400°F) mark 6 for about 20 minutes until golden brown. Leave to cool on a wire rack and serve while still fresh.

FARMHOUSE SULTANA CAKE

Serves 8

225 g (8 oz) plain flour
10 ml (2 tsp) mixed spice
5 ml (1 tsp) bicarbonate of soda
225 g (8 oz) plain wholemeal flour
175 g (6 oz) butter or block
  margarine
225 g (8 oz) soft dark brown sugar
225 g (8 oz) sultanas
1 egg, beaten
about 300 ml (½ pint) milk
10 sugar cubes

1 Grease and line a 20.5-cm (8-inch) square, loose bottomed cake tin.

2 Sift the plain flour, spice and bicarbonate of soda into a large bowl and stir in the wholemeal flour. Rub in the fat until the mixture resembles fine breadcrumbs and stir in the sugar and sultanas.

3 Make a well in the centre and gradually pour in the egg and milk. Beat gently until well mixed and of a soft dropping consistency, adding more milk if necessary.

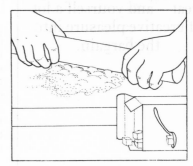

4 Turn the mixture into the prepared tin and level the surface. Roughly crush the sugar cubes with the end of a rolling pin and scatter over the cake.

5 Bake in the oven at 170°C (325°F) mark 3 for about 1 hour 40 minutes or until a fine, warmed skewer inserted into the centre comes out clean. Turn out to cool on a wire rack.

CREAMED CAKES

Cakes that contain half as much fat as flour, or more, are made by creaming the fat and sugar at the start. These cakes are rich and moist, firm to touch and they are excellent iced. They cut easily into fancy shapes, so make good children's party cakes.

Use butter or block margarine and take it out of the refrigerator a while before you want to use it. Choose a large mixing bowl, to give you room for vigorous beating and warm it a little to make creaming easier. Beat the fat and sugar together with a wooden spoon until they are as pale and fluffy as whipped cream. If the fat is a little hard to start with, beat it alone until well softened before adding the sugar. An electric mixer makes creaming easier.

Next beat in the eggs. These too should be at room temperature, and add them a little at a time to prevent curdling. If the mixture starts to curdle, add a little sifted flour with each portion of egg and beat in. Fold in the remaining flour with a large metal spoon.

Quicker to make than creamed cakes are those made by the 'all-in-one' method. For these you need soft 'tub' margarine, which is soft enough to beat straight from the refrigerator and which has been developed to give the best results with the 'all-in-one' method. You can use butter or block margarine but they must be soft; leave them at room temperature for at least 1 hour first.

For all-in-one cakes simply beat all the ingredients together with a wooden spoon for 2–3 minutes, or with a mixer for even less time. Use self-raising flour, to give the cake an extra boost, and caster or soft brown sugar, which dissolve quicker than other sugars.

The result of this method is a cake that is similar to one made by creaming, but it won't keep as well. Put it in an airtight container or wrap tightly in foil as soon as it is cold to prevent it going stale.

VICTORIA SANDWICH

Serves 6–8

100 g (4 oz) butter or block margarine
100 g (4 oz) caster sugar
2 eggs, beaten
100 g (4 oz) self-raising flour
caster sugar, to dredge
60 ml (4 tbsp) jam or 150 ml (5 fl oz) double cream, whipped or $\frac{1}{2}$ quantity butter cream (see page 154), to fill

1 Grease two 18-cm (7-inch) sandwich tins and line the base of each with greased greaseproof paper.

2 Put the fat and sugar into a warmed mixing bowl and cream together with a wooden spoon until pale and fluffy. Scrape mixture down from sides of bowl from time to time to ensure that no sugar crystals are left.

3 Add the egg a little at a time; beat well after each addition. Gradually sift the flour on to the mixture and fold it in as quickly and lightly as possible.

4 Place half the mixture in each of the prepared sandwich tins. Lightly smooth the surface of the mixture with a palette knife. Bake both cakes on the same shelf of the oven at 190°C (375°F) mark 5 for about 20 minutes until they are well risen and begin to shrink away from sides of tins.

5 Turn out and leave the cakes to cool on a wire rack, then sandwich them together with jam.

Chocolate sandwich Replace 45 ml (3 tbsp) flour with 45 ml (3 tbsp) cocoa powder. For a more moist cake, blend the cocoa with a little water to give a thick paste and beat it into the creamed ingredients with the eggs. Use chocolate butter cream as filling.

Coffee sandwich Dissolve 10 ml (2 tsp) instant coffee in a little water and add it to the creamed mixture with the egg, or use 10 ml (2 tsp) coffee essence. Use coffee butter cream as filling.

Orange or lemon sandwich Add the finely grated rind of one orange or lemon to the mixture and use orange or lemon curd or orange or lemon butter cream as filling. Use some of the juice from the orange or lemon to make glacé icing (see page 154).

Cup cakes Divide the mixture between 18 paper cases and bake as above. If liked, fold 50 g (2 oz) chocolate polka dots, sultanas, raisins, chopped walnuts or glacé cherries into the mixture with the

flour. When cold, top each cup cake with glacé icing (see page 154).

MADEIRA CAKE

Serves 6–8

100 g (4 oz) plain flour

100 g (4 oz) self-raising flour

175 g (6 oz) butter or block
  margarine

175 g (6 oz) caster sugar

5 ml (1 tsp) vanilla flavouring

3 eggs, beaten

15–30 ml (1–2 tbsp) milk
  (optional)

2–3 thin slices citron peel

1 Grease and line an 18-cm (7-inch) round cake tin. Sift the flours together.

2 Cream the butter or margarine and the sugar together until pale and fluffy, then beat in the vanilla flavouring.

3 Add the egg a little at a time, beating well after each addition.

4 Fold in the sifted flour with a metal spoon, adding a little milk if necessary to give a dropping consistency.

5 Turn the mixture into the prepared tin and bake in the oven at 180°C (350°F) mark 4 for 20 minutes.

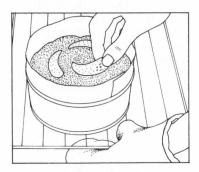

6 Lay the citron peel on top of the cake, return it to the oven and bake for a further 40 minutes until firm to the touch. Turn out and leave to cool on a wire rack.

CHOCOLATE BATTENBERG CAKE

Serves 10

175 g (6 oz) butter or margarine

175 g (6 oz) caster sugar

a few drops of vanilla flavouring

3 eggs, beaten

175 g (6 oz) self-raising flour

30 ml (2 tbsp) cocoa powder

a little milk, to mix (optional)

225 g (8 oz) almond paste

caster sugar, to dredge

225 g (8 oz) apricot jam, melted

1 Grease and line a 30 × 20.5-cm (12 × 8-inch) Swiss roll tin and divide it lengthways with a 'wall' of greaseproof paper.

2 Cream fat and sugar together until pale and fluffy, then beat in vanilla flavouring. Add the egg a little at a time, beating well.

3 Gradually sift the flour over the mixture and fold it in lightly. Turn half the mixture into one side of the tin and level the surface. Sift the cocoa over the other half and fold in, adding a little milk if necessary to give a dropping consistency.

4 Turn the chocolate mixture into the tin and level surface. Bake in the oven at 190°C (375°F) mark 5 for 40–45 minutes until well risen and firm. Turn out and leave to cool on a wire rack.

5 When cold, trim cakes to an equal size and cut each in half lengthways. On a working surface sprinkled with caster sugar, roll out the almond paste to a 30-cm (12-inch) square.

6 Place one strip of cake on the almond paste so that it lies up against the edge of paste. Place an alternate coloured strip next to it.

7 Brush top and sides of cake with melted jam and layer up with alternate coloured strips.

8 Bring almond paste up and over cake to cover it. Press paste firmly on to cake, then seal and trim join. Place cake seam-side down and trim both ends with a sharp knife. Crimp top edges of paste with the thumb and forefinger and mark the top in a criss-cross pattern with a knife. Dredge lightly with caster sugar.

APPLE CAKE

Serves 8

350 g (12 oz) self-raising flour

2.5 ml ($\frac{1}{2}$ tsp) salt

5 ml (1 tsp) ground cinnamon

2.5 ml ($\frac{1}{2}$ tsp) ground nutmeg

2.5 ml ($\frac{1}{2}$ tsp) ground cloves

5 ml (1 tsp) bicarbonate of
  soda

450 ml ($\frac{3}{4}$ pint) apple purée

100 g (4 oz) butter or block
  margarine

175 g (6 oz) light brown soft sugar

1 egg, separated

100 g (4 oz) seedless raisins

1 Grease and line with greased greaseproof paper a 20.5-cm (8-inch) round cake tin. Sift together the flour, salt and spices.

2 Add the bicarbonate of soda to the apple purée and stir until dissolved.

3 Cream the butter or margarine and the sugar together until pale and fluffy, then beat in the egg yolk.

4 Fold in the flour and apple purée alternately, then stir in the seedless raisins.

5 Whisk the egg white until stiff, and fold in with a large metal spoon.

6 Turn the mixture into the prepared tin. Bake in the oven at 180°C (350°F) mark 4 for about 1–1$\frac{1}{2}$ hours until firm to the touch. Turn out and leave to cool on a wire rack.

RICH FRUIT CAKES

A rich fruit cake is traditional for family celebrations. At weddings and Christenings, anniversaries and Christmas, the centrepiece will most often be a beautiful cake decorated with royal icing; beneath the sugar coating will be a dark, glossy cake loaded with fruit, candied peel, nuts and spices and deliciously soaked with brandy.

Like other rich cakes, fruit cakes are made by the creaming method (see page 136), but the mixture is slightly stiffer to support the weight of the fruit. If the mixture is too wet fruit is inclined to sink to the bottom. Remember that all dried fruit should be thoroughly cleaned and dried before use; glacé cherries should be rinsed to remove excess syrup, then dried. Toss all fruit in a little of the measured flour.

You will find that creaming and mixing a rich fruit cake is quite hard work, especially if it is a large cake, and the baking times are long. So it is useful to know that you can mix one day and bake the next if it is more convenient. Put the prepared mixture in the tin, cover it loosely with a clean cloth and leave it in a cool place until you are ready to bake.

Protect the outside of a rich fruit cake from overbrowning during the long cooking by wrapping a double thickness of brown paper round the outside of the tin. Stand the tin on several thicknesses of brown paper or newspaper in the oven and cover the top of the cake towards the end of cooking if necessary.

All fruit cakes keep well, but the richest actually improve if kept for two or three months before you cut them. When the cake is cold, wrap it in greaseproof paper and put it in an airtight container or wrap in foil; every two or three weeks, get it out, prick the surface with a fine skewer and spoon over a little brandy or other spirit.

RICH FRUIT CAKE
(see quantity chart, opposite)

1 Grease and line the cake tin for the size of cake you wish to make, using a double thickness of greaseproof paper. Tie a double band of brown paper round the outside.

2 Prepare the ingredients for the appropriate size of cake according to the chart opposite. Wash and dry all the fruit, if necessary chopping any over-large pieces, and mix well together in a large bowl. Add the flaked almonds. Sift flour and spices into another bowl with a pinch of salt.

3 Put the butter, sugar and lemon rind into a warmed mixing bowl and cream together with a wooden spoon until pale and fluffy. Add the beaten eggs, a little at a time, beating well after each addition.

4 Gradually fold the flour lightly into the mixture with a metal spoon, then fold in the brandy. Finally fold in the fruit and nuts.

5 Turn the mixture into the prepared tin, spreading it evenly and making sure there are no air pockets. Make a hollow in the centre to ensure an even surface when cooked.

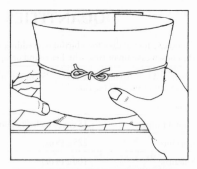

6 Stand the tin on newspaper or brown paper in the oven and bake at 150°C (300°F) mark 2 for the required time (see chart), until a fine skewer inserted in the centre comes out clean. To prevent the cake from overbrowning, cover it with greaseproof paper after about 1½ hours.

7 When cooked, leave the cake to cool in the tin before turning out on to a wire rack. Prick the top of the cake all over with a fine skewer and slowly pour 30–45 ml (2–3 tbsp) brandy over it before storing.

8 Wrap the cake in a double thickness of greaseproof paper and place upside down in an airtight tin. Cover with foil to store.

QUANTITIES AND SIZES FOR RICH FRUIT CAKES

To make a formal cake for a birthday, wedding or anniversary, the following chart will show you the amount of ingredients required to fill the chosen cake tin or tins, whether round or square.

* Note   When baking large cakes, 25 cm (10 inches) and upwards, it is advisable to reduce the oven heat to 130°C (250°F) mark $\frac{1}{2}$ after two-thirds of the cooking time.

Square tin size		15 cm (6 inches) square	18 cm (7 inches) square	20.5 cm (8 inches) square
Round tin size	15 cm (6 inches) diameter	18 cm (7 inches) diameter	20.5 cm (8 inches) diameter	23 cm (9 inches) diameter
Currants	225 g (8 oz)	350 g (12 oz)	450 g (1 lb)	625 g (1 lb 6 oz)
Sultanas	100 g (4 oz)	125 g (4$\frac{1}{2}$ oz)	200 g (7 oz)	225 g (8 oz)
Raisins	100 g (4 oz)	125 g (4$\frac{1}{2}$ oz)	200 g (7 oz)	225 g (8 oz)
Glacé cherries	50 g (2 oz)	75 g (3 oz)	150 g (5 oz)	175 g (6 oz)
Mixed peel	25 g (1 oz)	50 g (2 oz)	75 g (3 oz)	100 g (4 oz)
Flaked almonds	25 g (1 oz)	50 g (2 oz)	75 g (3 oz)	100 g (4 oz)
Lemon rind	a little	a little	a little	$\frac{1}{4}$ lemon
Plain flour	175 g (6 oz)	215 g (7$\frac{1}{2}$ oz)	350 g (12 oz)	400 g (14 oz)
Mixed spice	1.25 ml ($\frac{1}{4}$ tsp)	2.5 ml ($\frac{1}{2}$ tsp)	2.5 ml ($\frac{1}{2}$ tsp)	5 ml (1 tsp)
Cinnamon	1.25 ml ($\frac{1}{4}$ tsp)	2.5 ml ($\frac{1}{2}$ tsp)	2.5 ml ($\frac{1}{2}$ tsp)	5 ml (1 tsp)
Butter	150 g (5 oz)	175 g (6 oz)	275 g (10 oz)	350 g (12 oz)
Sugar	150 g (5 oz)	175 g (6 oz)	275 g (10 oz)	350 g (12 oz)
Eggs, beaten	2$\frac{1}{2}$	3	5	6
Brandy	15 ml (1 tbsp)	15 ml (1 tbsp)	15–30 ml (1–2 tbsp)	30 ml (2 tbsp)
Time (approx.)	2$\frac{1}{2}$–3 hours	3 hours	3$\frac{1}{2}$ hours	4 hours
Weight when cooked	1.1 kg (2$\frac{1}{2}$ lb)	1.6 kg (3$\frac{1}{4}$ lb)	2.2 kg (4$\frac{3}{4}$ lb)	2.7 kg (6 lb)

Square tin size	23 cm (9 inches) square	25.5 cm (10 inches) square	28 cm (11 inches) square	30.5 cm (12 inches) square
Round tin size	25.5 cm (10 inches) diameter	28 cm (11 inches) diameter	30.5 cm (12 inches) diameter	
Currants	775 g (1 lb 12 oz)	1.1 kg (2 lb 8 oz)	1.5 kg (3 lb 2 oz)	1.7 kg (3 lb 12 oz)
Sultanas	375 g (13 oz)	400 g (14 oz)	525 g (1 lb 3 oz)	625 g (1 lb 6 oz)
Raisins	375 g (13 oz)	400 g (14 oz)	525 g (1 lb 3 oz)	625 g (1 lb 6 oz)
Glacé cherries	250 g (9 oz)	275 g (10 oz)	350 g (12 oz)	425 g (15 oz)
Mixed peel	150 g (5 oz)	200 g (7 oz)	250 g (9 oz)	275 g (10 oz)
Flaked almonds	150 g (5 oz)	200 g (7 oz)	250 g (9 oz)	275 g (10 oz)
Lemon rind	$\frac{1}{4}$ lemon	$\frac{1}{2}$ lemon	$\frac{1}{2}$ lemon	1 lemon
Plain flour	600 g (1 lb 5 oz)	700 g (1 lb 8 oz)	825 g (1 lb 13 oz)	1 kg (2 lb 6 oz)
Mixed spice	5 ml (1 tsp)	10 ml (2 tsp)	12.5 ml (2$\frac{1}{2}$ tsp)	12.5 ml (2$\frac{1}{2}$ tsp)
Cinnamon	5 ml (1 tsp)	10 ml (2 tsp)	12.5 ml (2$\frac{1}{2}$ tsp)	12.5 ml (2$\frac{1}{2}$ tsp)
Butter	500 g (1 lb 2 oz)	600 g (1 lb 5 oz)	800 g (1 lb 12 oz)	950 g (2 lb 2 oz)
Sugar	500 g (1 lb 2 oz)	600 g (1 lb 5 oz)	800 g (1 lb 12 oz)	950 g (2 lb 2 oz)
Eggs, beaten	9	11	14	17
Brandy	30–45 ml (2–3 tbsp)	45 ml (3 tbsp)	60 ml (4 tbsp)	90 ml (6 tbsp)
Time (approx.)	6 hours	7 hours	8 hours	8$\frac{1}{2}$ hours
Weight when cooked	4 kg (9 lb)	5.2 kg (11$\frac{1}{2}$ lb)	6.7 kg (14$\frac{3}{4}$ lb)	7.7 kg (17 lb)

MERINGUES

If you want the simplest possible cake for a special tea or dessert, a meringue is a good choice. Light as air and sweet as sugar, they are easy to make and few people can refuse them.

All meringues are based on stiffly whisked egg whites. The most common type is made by folding in caster sugar; when baked this gives a crisp, off-white meringue with a very slightly soft inside. It can be formed into rounds or mounds or piped—either in the traditional 'shell' shape or in nests to hold fruit or cream fillings. Using the same method but substituting icing sugar gives a much drier, whiter meringue. For a firm meringue for elaborate baskets, the sugar is added in the form of a hot syrup. Finally, a really soft meringue can be made by adding a little vinegar and cornflour. This is used to make a pavlova.

Meringues are best made with eggs that are 2–3 days old. Separate the whites from the yolks carefully, making sure that no trace of yolk gets into the whites. If possible, keep the separated whites in a covered container in the refrigerator for up to 24 hours before use—this makes them more gelatinous and whisk more quickly to a greater volume. Otherwise use them straight after separating, but the colder the better; a pinch of salt or cream of tartar can be added to help them hold their shape.

Whisk until the whites are stiff enough to stand in peaks, then add the sugar. For a basic meringue, whisk in half the sugar first, then fold the rest in lightly with a large metal spoon. Shape the meringue quickly, before the mixture separates, on a baking sheet lined with non-stick paper. Dry out or bake in a low oven for several hours until crisp. When cool, store in an airtight container; meringues keep well unfilled for 2–3 weeks; they also freeze very successfully in rigid polythene containers.

SMALL MERINGUES

2 egg whites
100 g (4 oz) caster sugar
150 ml (5 fl oz) double cream

1 Line a large baking sheet with non-stick paper. Whisk the egg whites until very stiff.

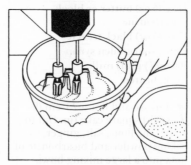

2 Add half the sugar and whisk again until the mixture regains its former stiffness. Fold the remaining sugar into the mixture very lightly with a metal spoon.

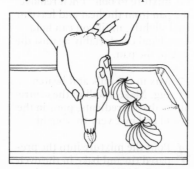

3 Spoon the mixture into a piping bag fitted with a large star nozzle and pipe small mounds on to the prepared baking sheet.

4 Dry out in the oven at 130°C (250°F) mark ½ for 2–3 hours until the meringues are firm and crisp but still white. If they begin to colour, prop the oven door open slightly. Ease the meringues off the paper and leave to cool on a wire rack. Whip cream until stiff and use to sandwich meringues in pairs.

MOCHA MERINGUE

3 egg whites
175 g (6 oz) caster sugar
15 ml (1 tbsp) instant coffee powder
For the filling
300 ml (10 fl oz) double cream
2 egg whites
5 ml (1 tsp) instant coffee powder
25 g (1 oz) chocolate, grated
25 g (1 oz) almonds, finely chopped
chopped almonds and grated chocolate, to decorate

1 Draw two 20.5-cm (8-inch) circles on non-stick paper and place on two baking sheets.

2 Whisk the egg whites until very stiff. Whisk in half the sugar, add the instant coffee and whisk until the mixture is really stiff and no longer speckled with coffee. Carefully fold in the remaining sugar with a metal spoon.

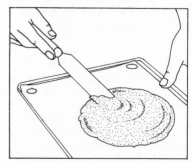

3 Divide the mixture between the baking sheets and spread evenly to fill the circles. Bake in the oven at 150°C (300°F) mark 2 for about 2 hours until dry. Leave to cool on the baking sheets before carefully lifting them off.

4 To make up the filling, whip the cream until thick. Whisk the egg whites until stiff, then carefully fold into the cream. Fold in the coffee, chocolate and nuts.

5 Sandwich the meringue layers together with half the cream mixture. Spread remainder on top; decorate with nuts and chocolate 30 minutes before serving.

MELTED CAKES

If honey, treacle, syrup or chocolate are included in a recipe, the cake is made by melting these ingredients with the sugar and fat before mixing with the flour. This ensures that they blend in evenly. The result is a cake with a moist and irresistibly sticky texture. The method is a very easy one, traditionally used for gingerbreads and American brownies.

The raising agent in cakes made by this method is usually bicarbonate of soda, which reacts with the natural acids present in liquid sweeteners, and spices are often added to enhance the flavour and counteract any soda taste.

Measure treacle, syrup and honey carefully, as too much of these products can cause a heavy, sunken cake. Warm the fat, sugar and liquid sweetener gently, just until the sugar is dissolved and the fat melted. Do not let the mixture boil or it will be unusable.

Let the mixture cool slightly and add any other liquids such as milk and eggs before adding to the flour. If a hot liquid is added to the flour, it will begin to cook and the cake will be hard.

If the recipe includes chocolate, break the chocolate into a bowl and add the fat, cut into pieces. Place the bowl over a saucepan of hot, but not boiling, water and heat it gently until melted. The chocolate and butter should blend to a smooth cream when stirred together. Let it cool a little before adding to the flour.

The final mixture will be a thick, heavy batter that can be poured into the tin. It will not need smoothing, as it will find its own level. Cakes made by this method are generally baked at a low to moderate temperature until just risen and firm to the touch. They are best left for a day or two before cutting, to allow the crust to soften and the flavour to mellow, and they keep well if stored in an airtight container.

GINGERBREAD

Serves 8–10

450 g (1 lb) plain flour
5 ml (1 tsp) salt
15 ml (1 tbsp) ground ginger
15 ml (1 tbsp) baking powder
5 ml (1 tsp) bicarbonate of soda
225 g (8 oz) demerara sugar
175 g (6 oz) butter or block margarine
175 g (6 oz) black treacle
175 g (6 oz) golden syrup
300 ml ($\frac{1}{2}$ pint) milk
1 egg, beaten

1 Grease and line a 23-cm (9-inch) square cake tin. Sift together the flour, salt, ginger, baking powder and bicarbonate of soda into a large mixing bowl.

2 Put the sugar, fat, treacle and syrup in a saucepan and warm gently over a low heat until melted and well blended. Do not allow the mixture to boil. Then remove the pan from the heat and leave to cool slightly, until you can hold your hand comfortably against the side of the pan.

3 Mix in the milk and beaten egg. Make a well in the centre of the dry ingredients, pour in the liquid and mix very thoroughly.

4 Pour the mixture into the prepared tin and bake in the oven at 170°C (325°F) mark 3 for about 1$\frac{1}{2}$ hours until firm but springy to the touch.

5 Leave the gingerbread in the tin for about 10 minutes after baking, then turn out on to a wire rack, remove the lining paper and leave to cool.

BOSTON BROWNIES

Makes about 16

50 g (2 oz) plain chocolate
65 g (2$\frac{1}{2}$ oz) butter or block margarine
175 g (6 oz) caster sugar
65 g (2$\frac{1}{2}$ oz) self-raising flour
1.25 ml ($\frac{1}{4}$ tsp) salt
2 eggs, beaten
2.5 ml ($\frac{1}{2}$ tsp) vanilla flavouring
50 g (2 oz) walnuts, roughly chopped

1 Grease and line a shallow 20.5-cm (8-inch) square cake tin. Then break up the chocolate and put it in a bowl with the butter, cut into pieces. Stand the bowl over a pan of hot water and heat gently, stirring occasionally, until melted. Add the caster sugar.

2 Sift together the flour and salt into a bowl. Add the chocolate mixture, eggs, vanilla flavouring and walnuts. Mix thoroughly.

3 Pour the mixture into the prepared tin and bake in the oven at 180°C (350°F) mark 4 for 35–40 minutes until the mixture is risen and just beginning to leave the sides of the cake tin.

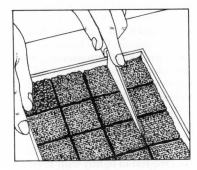

4 Leave in the tin to cool, then cut the Boston brownies into squares with a sharp knife.

SPONGE CAKES

The classic sponge cake is light and feathery, made by whisking together eggs and caster sugar, then folding in the flour. There is no fat in the mixture, and the cake rises simply because of the air incorporated during whisking. For an even lighter cake the egg yolks and sugar can be whisked together, with the whites whisked separately and folded in afterwards.

The whisking method produces the lightest of all cakes. Sponges are perfect for filling with whipped cream and fruit and are used for many gâteaux, dessert cakes and for Swiss rolls. Because they have no fat they always need a filling, and they do not keep well. Bake a sponge the day you wish to eat it.

A moister version of a whisked sponge is a Genoese sponge. This is also made by the whisking method, but melted butter is added with the flour. This gives a delicate sponge, lighter than a Victoria sandwich, but with a moister texture than the plain whisked sponge, and a delicious buttery taste. Don't try to substitute margarine for butter in this recipe or the flavour and texture will be lost. A Genoese sponge keeps better than a plain whisked sponge.

To make a really good sponge, don't rush. The eggs and sugar must be whisked until thick enough to leave a trail when the whisk is lifted from the surface. If you use a rotary whisk or a hand-held electric mixer, place the bowl over a saucepan of hot water to speed the thickening process and make it less hard work. Do not let the bottom of the bowl touch the water or the mixture will become too hot. When the mixture is really thick and double in volume, take the bowl off the heat and continue to whisk until it is cool.

Add the flour carefully. Sift it first, then add a little at a time to the whisked mixture and fold it in until evenly blended. Do not stir or you will break the air bubbles and the cake will not rise.

WHISKED SPONGE CAKE

Serves 6–8

3 eggs, size 2

100 g (4 oz) caster sugar

75 g (3 oz) plain flour

1 Grease and line two 18-cm (7-inch) sandwich tins and dust with a little flour or with a mixture of flour and caster sugar.

2 Put the eggs and sugar in a large deep bowl and stand it over a pan of hot water. The bowl should fit snugly over the pan and the bottom of the bowl should not touch the bottom of the pan.

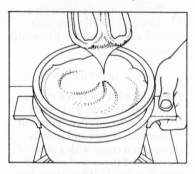

Whisk the eggs and sugar together until doubled in volume and thick enough to leave a trail on the surface when the whisk is lifted. If whisking by hand, this will take 15–20 minutes; if a hand-held electric mixer is used, 7–10 minutes will be enough.

3 Remove the bowl from the heat and continue whisking for a further 5 minutes until the mixture is cooler and creamy looking.

4 Sift half the flour over the mixture and fold it in very lightly, using a large metal spoon. Sift and fold in the remaining flour in the same way.

5 Pour the mixture into the prepared tins, tilting the tins to spread the mixture evenly. Do not use a palette knife or spatula to smooth the mixture as this will crush out the air bubbles.

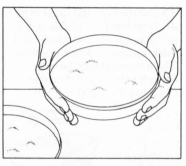

6 Bake the cakes in the oven at 190°C (375°F) mark 5 for 20–25 minutes until firm but springy to the touch. Turn out and leave to cool on a wire rack for 30 minutes.

7 When the cakes are cold, sandwich them together with strawberry or apricot jam, whipped cream or butter cream and dredge with caster sugar or cover the top with glacé icing (see page 154).

SWISS ROLL

Serves 6–8

3 eggs, size 2

100 g (4 oz) caster sugar

100 g (4 oz) plain flour

15 ml (1 tbsp) hot water

caster sugar, to dredge

100 g (4 oz) jam, warmed

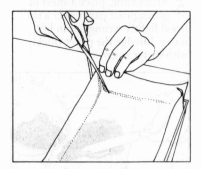

1 Grease a 33 × 23 cm (13 × 9 inch) Swiss roll tin. Cut a piece of greaseproof paper about 5 cm (2 inches) larger all round than the tin. Place it on the tin, creasing it to fit, and make cuts from corners of paper to corners of creases. Put in tin and grease.

2 Put the eggs and sugar in a large bowl, stand this over a pan of hot water and whisk until thick, creamy and pale in colour. The mixture should be stiff enough to leave a trail on the surface when the whisk is lifted.

3 Remove the bowl from the heat and whisk until cool. Sift half the flour over the mixture and fold in very lightly with a metal spoon. Sift and fold in the remaining flour, then lightly stir in the hot water.

4 Pour the mixture into the prepared tin and tilt the tin backwards and forwards to spread the mixture in an even layer. Bake in the oven at 220°C (425°F) mark 7 for 7–9 minutes until golden brown, well risen and firm to the touch.

5 Meanwhile, place a sheet of greaseproof paper over a tea towel lightly wrung out in hot water. Dredge the paper thickly with caster sugar.

6 Quickly turn out the cake on to the paper, trim off the crusty edges; spread with warmed jam.

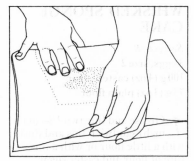

7 Roll up the cake with the aid of the paper. Make the first turn firmly so that the whole cake will roll evenly and have a good shape when finished, but roll more lightly after this turn.

8 Place seam-side down on a wire rack and dredge with sugar. Leave to cool for 30 minutes before serving.

——————— VARIATION ———————

Chocolate Swiss roll Replace 15 ml (1 tbsp) flour with 15 ml (1 tbsp) cocoa powder. Turn out the cooked sponge and trim as above, then cover with a sheet of greaseproof paper and roll with the paper inside. When the cake is cold, unroll and remove the paper. Spread with whipped cream or butter cream and re-roll. Dust with icing sugar.

GENOESE SPONGE

Serves 6–8

40 g (1½ oz) butter
3 eggs, size 2
75 g (3 oz) caster sugar
65 g (2½ oz) plain flour
15 ml (1 tbsp) cornflour

1 Grease and line two 18-cm (7-inch) sandwich tins or one 18-cm (7-inch) deeper cake tin.

2 Put the butter into a saucepan and heat gently until melted, then remove from the heat and leave to stand for a few minutes to cool slightly.

3 Put the eggs and sugar in a bowl, stand it over a pan of hot water and whisk until thick, creamy and pale in colour. The mixture should be stiff enough to leave a trail on the surface when the whisk is lifted. Remove from the heat and continue whisking until cool.

4 Sift the flours together into a bowl. Fold half the flour into the egg mixture with a metal spoon.

5 Pour half the cooled butter round the edge of the mixture. Gradually fold in the remaining butter and flour alternately. Be sure to fold in very lightly or the fat will sink to the bottom and cause a heavy cake.

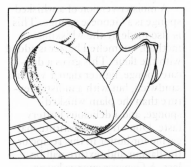

6 Pour the mixture into the prepared tins. Bake sandwich cakes in the oven at 180°C (350°F) mark 4 for 25–30 minutes, or a deep cake for 35–40 minutes, until golden brown and firm to the touch. Turn out and leave to cool on a wire rack for 30 minutes before serving.

——————— VARIATION ———————

Chocolate Genoese For either cake, replace 15 g (½ oz) plain flour with 15 g (½ oz) cocoa powder.

YEAST CAKES

Cakes baked with yeast have a magic of their own. The lively rising of the dough before it is cooked and the characteristic yeasty smell during baking make this type of baking a special pleasure.

Fresh and dried yeast give equally good flavour and texture to the finished cake; only the method of using them is different. Fresh yeast is rather like putty in colour and texture and should crumble easily when broken. Although it will store for up to 1 week wrapped in foil in the refrigerator or for up to 3 months in the freezer, it will give best results when absolutely fresh, so buy it in small quantities when required. Dried yeast keeps well in an airtight container in a cool dry place for at least 6 months.

Yeast needs warmth in which to grow, so all the cake ingredients should be at warm room temperature. When using fresh yeast, blend it with tepid liquid (which feels warm when tested with a little finger) before adding to the flour. Dried yeast must be activated in advance by mixing with a proportion of the recipe liquid (usually a third) and a little sugar; leave for 15 minutes before use.

In plain mixtures the yeast liquid can be blended straight into the flour and fat, kneaded and left to rise. Rich mixtures containing larger proportions of fat and eggs retard the growth of the yeast, so to help it you start it off with a 'sponge batter'. This is made with about a third of the flour and all the liquid; the yeast is blended into the batter and it is left until frothy before blending with remaining ingredients. With the sponge batter method there is no need to activate dried yeast ahead.

Always use strong flour for recipes made with yeast; the extra gluten helps give the cake a light, open texture. With a plain mixture, kneading will help develop the gluten and give a better rise.

DOUGHNUTS

Makes 10–12

15 g (½ oz) fresh yeast or 10 ml (2 tsp) dried yeast
about 60 ml (4 tbsp) tepid milk
pinch of sugar (optional)
225 g (8 oz) strong plain flour
2.5 ml (½ tsp) salt
knob of butter or block margarine
1 egg, beaten
jam
fat, for deep frying
sugar and ground cinnamon

1 If using dried yeast sprinkle it on the milk and add the sugar; leave for about 15 minutes until frothy. If using fresh yeast, just blend it with the milk.

2 Sift the flour and salt into a bowl and rub in the fat. Add the yeast liquid and egg and mix to a soft dough, adding a little more milk if necessary. Beat well until smooth. Cover with a clean cloth and leave to rise in a warm place until doubled in size.

3 Knead lightly on a lightly floured working surface and divide into ten–twelve pieces.

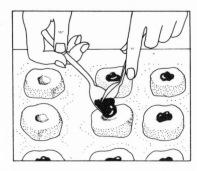

4 Shape each piece into a round, with a small hole in the middle. Put 5 ml (1 tsp) jam in the centre and draw up edges to form a ball.

5 Heat the fat to 180°C (360°F) or until it will brown a 2.5-cm (1-inch) cube of bread in 1 minute. Fry the doughnuts for 5–10 minutes until golden. Drain and toss in sugar mixed with cinnamon.

RUM BABAS

Makes 16

25 g (1 oz) fresh yeast or 15 ml (1 tbsp) dried
90 ml (6 tbsp) tepid milk
225 g (8 oz) strong plain flour
2.5 ml (½ tsp) salt
30 ml (2 tbsp) caster sugar
4 eggs, beaten
100 g (4 oz) butter, softened
100 g (4 oz) currants
300 ml (10 fl oz) double cream
120 ml (8 tbsp) clear honey
120 ml (8 tbsp) water
a little rum

1 Lightly grease sixteen 9-cm (3½-inch) ring tins with lard and place them on baking sheets.

2 Put the yeast, milk and 50 g (2 oz) flour into a bowl and blend until smooth. Cover with a clean cloth and leave in a warm place for 15 minutes until frothy.

3 Add the remaining flour, the salt, sugar, eggs, butter and currants and beat well with a wooden spoon for 3–4 minutes.

4 Half-fill the prepared tins with the dough, cover with a cloth and leave to rise in a warm place until tins are two-thirds full.

5 Bake in the oven at 200°C (400°C) mark 6 for 15–20 minutes until well risen, golden and just beginning to shrink away from the sides of the tins. Leave to cool in the tins for a few minutes.

6 Meanwhile, make the rum syrup. Put the honey and water together in a pan and warm gently. Add rum to taste.

7 Turn the rum babas out on to a wire rack and put a tray underneath. While the babas are still hot, spoon rum syrup over each one until well soaked. Cool. To serve, whip the cream until thick and spoon or pipe some in to the centre of each baba.

WHAT WENT WRONG

Too close a texture
1 Too much liquid.
2 Too little raising agent.
3 Insufficient creaming of the fat and sugar–air should be well incorporated at this stage.
4 Curdling of the creamed mixture when the eggs are added (a curdled mixture holds less air than one of the correct consistency).
5 Over-stirring or beating the flour into a creamed mixture when little or no raising agent is present.

Uneven texture with holes
1 Over-stirring or uneven mixing in of the flour.
2 Putting the mixture into the cake tin in small amounts—pockets of air trapped in the mixture.

Dry and crumbly texture
1 Too much raising agent.
2 Too long a cooking time in too cool an oven.

Fruit cakes dry and crumbly
1 Cooking at too high a temperature.
2 Too stiff a mixture.
3 Not lining the tin thoroughly—for a large cake, double greaseproof paper should be used.

Fruit sinking to the bottom of the cake
1 Damp fruit.
2 Sticky glacé cherries.
3 Too soft a mixture: a rich fruit cake mixture should be fairly stiff, so that it can support the weight of the fruit.
4 Opening or banging the oven door while the cake is rising.
5 Using self-raising flour where the recipe requires plain, or using too much baking powder—the cake over-rises and cannot carry the fruit with it.

'Peaking' and 'cracking'
1 Too hot an oven.
2 The cake being placed too near top of the oven.
3 Too stiff a mixture.
4 Too small a cake tin.

Close, heavy-textured whisked sponge
1 The eggs and sugar being insufficiently beaten, so that not enough air is enclosed.
2 The flour being stirred in too heavily or for too long—very light folding movements are required and a metal spoon should be used.

Cakes sinking in the middle
1 Too soft a mixture.
2 Too much raising agent.
3 Too cool an oven, which means that the centre of the cake does not rise.
4 Too hot an oven, which makes the cake appear to be done on the outside before it is cooked through, so that it is taken from the oven too soon.
5 Insufficient baking.

Burnt fruit on the outside of a fruit cake
1 Too high a temperature.
2 Lack of protection: as soon as the cake begins to colour, a piece of brown paper or a double thickness of greaseproof paper should be placed over the top for the remainder of the cooking time to prevent further browning.

A heavy layer at the base of a Genoese sponge
1 The melted fat being too hot—it should be only lukewarm and just flowing.
2 Uneven or insufficient folding in of fat or flour.
3 Pouring the fat into the centre of the mixture instead of round the edge.

DISGUISING THE DAMAGE

If a cake goes wrong in the baking, there is no way of going back and putting it right without baking a new cake. But there are ways of disguising the damage so that only you will know.

● If a chocolate cake turns out rather too moist, call it a pudding and serve it with a fluffy sauce.

● If homemade biscuits crumble badly, use them to make a biscuit crumb flan case.

● If the top of a fruit cake gets burnt, cut it off and use a well flavoured almond paste to disguise it.

● If meringues break as you lift them off the baking sheet, serve large pieces on top of fruit and cream.

● If a sponge cake turns out a thin, flat layer, cut into fancy shapes with a biscuit cutter and sandwich together with jam and cream.

● If your cake rises unevenly, level the top, turn it over and ice the bottom.

● If a cake breaks as you take it out of the tin, disguise it as a pudding with custard sauce or fruit.

● If a cake sinks in the middle, cut out the centre and turn it into a ring cake. Ice it with butter cream or almond paste and royal icing, according to type, or decorate with whipped cream and fill the centre with fruit for a dessert.

● If a sponge or plain cake is dry, crumbly or heavy, use it as the base for a trifle and soak it in plenty of booze!

Perfect Pastry and Biscuits

There is no doubt that making your own pastry does take time, but the end results are usually worth it. There are many different types of pastry and each has its own distinctive texture, flavour and use. The art of producing good pastry lies in understanding the basic rules by which each one is made and sticking to them.

PASTRY CAKES

For successful pastry, work in a cool kitchen with cool utensils and ingredients. As you work, handle the pastry as little as possible and use just your finger and thumb tips for rubbing in fat.

For most pastries, use plain flour. For puff pastry use strong flour, to help give it a light, open structure. Butter and block margarine are interchangeable in short pastries, and give good results when mixed with lard. Proprietary vegetable shortenings and pure vegetable oils can also be used, but follow the manufacturer's directions as the quantities required may be less. In richer pastries stick to butter. Add liquid to a pastry mixture gradually, using just enough to bind it.

Pâte sucrée is a really rich shortcrust that keeps its shape well; use it for continental pâtisseries. *Shortcrust* is probably the most widely used pastry, and is quick and easy to prepare. *Flan pastry* is a slightly richer pastry made by the same method. It is usually sweetened, and it is ideal for flans.

Puff pastry is the richest of all and rises to layer upon layer of crisp, delicate flakes. Because it takes so long to make most people make it only occasionally, making up a large batch and freezing it in small quantities for future use.

Flaky pastry is used where a rich pastry is required but when the rise is not so important. *Rough puff* is quicker and easier to make and similar in appearance to flaky, but the texture is not so even.

Choux pastry is made by melting the fat and beating in the flour and the resulting paste is piped to shape. The result is a light, crisp shell, almost hollow inside.

* When a recipe states 225 g (8 oz) pastry, use pastry made with 225 g (8 oz) flour. If using bought pastry, buy a packet weighing twice that amount.

PÂTE SUCRÉE

100 g (4 oz) plain flour
pinch of salt
50 g (2 oz) caster sugar
50 g (2 oz) butter, at room temperature
2 egg yolks

1 Sift the flour and salt together on to a working surface or, preferably, a marble slab.

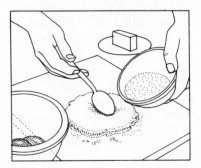

2 Make a well in the centre of the mixture and add the sugar, butter and egg yolks.

3 Using the fingertips of one hand, pinch and work the sugar, butter and egg yolks together until well blended. Gradually work in all the flour, adding a little water if necessary to bind it together.

4 Knead lightly until smooth, then wrap the pastry in foil or cling film and leave to 'rest' in the refrigerator or a cool place for about 1 hour.

5 Roll out the pastry on a lightly floured surface and use as required. *Pâte sucrée* is usually cooked at 190°C (375°F) mark 5.

SHORTCRUST PASTRY

175 g (6 oz) plain flour
pinch of salt
75 g (3 oz) butter or block margarine and lard
about 30 ml (2 tbsp) cold water

1 Mix the flour and salt together in a bowl. Cut the fat into small pieces and add it to the flour.

2 Using both hands, rub the fat into the flour between finger and thumb tips until the mixture resembles fine breadcrumbs.

3 Add the water, sprinkling it evenly over the surface. Stir it in with a round-bladed knife until the mixture begins to stick together in large lumps.

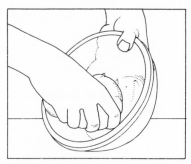

4 With one hand, collect the mixture together and knead lightly for a few seconds to give a firm, smooth dough. The pastry can be used straight away, but is better allowed to 'rest' for about 30 minutes. It can also be wrapped in cling film and kept in the refrigerator for a day or two.

5 *To roll out:* sprinkle a very little flour on a working surface and the rolling pin, not on the pastry, and roll out the dough evenly in one direction only, turning it occasionally. The ideal thickness is usually about 0.3 cm ($\frac{1}{8}$ inch). Do not pull or stretch the pastry. When cooking shortcrust pastry, the usual oven temperature is 200–220°C (400–425°F) mark 6–7.

FLAN PASTRY

100 g (4 oz) plain flour
pinch of salt
75 g (3 oz) butter or block margarine and lard
5 ml (1 tsp) caster sugar
1 egg, beaten

1 Mix the flour and salt together in a bowl. Cut the fat into small pieces, add it to the flour and rub it in as for shortcrust pastry until the mixture resembles fine breadcrumbs. Stir in the sugar.

2 Add the egg, stirring with a round-bladed knife until the ingredients begin to stick together in large lumps.

3 With one hand, collect the mixture together and knead lightly for a few seconds to give a firm, smooth dough.

4 Roll out as for shortcrust pastry and use as required. When cooking flan pastry the usual oven temperature is 200°C (400°F) mark 6.

BAKING BLIND

Baking blind is the process of baking a pastry case without the filling—essential if the filling is to be uncooked or if it only requires a short cooking time. First shape the pastry into the baking tin. Prick the pastry base with a fork. For large cases, cut a round of greaseproof paper rather larger

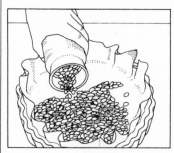

than the tin. Use this to line the pastry and weight it down with some dried beans, pasta or rice. Alternatively, screw up a piece of foil and use that to line the base of the pastry case. Bake the pastry at the temperature given in the recipe for 10–15 minutes, then remove the baking beans and paper or foil lining and return the tin to the oven for a further 5 minutes to crisp the pastry. Leave the baked case to cool and shrink slightly before removing it from the tin. (The baking beans can be kept for use again.)

For small cases, it is usually sufficient to prick the pastry well with a fork before baking.

Baked unfilled pastry cases can be kept for a few days in an airtight container.

ROUGH PUFF PASTRY

225 g (8 oz) plain flour
pinch of salt
75 g (3 oz) butter or block margarine
75 g (3 oz) lard
about 150 ml ($\frac{1}{4}$ pint) cold water
a squeeze of lemon juice
beaten egg, to glaze

1 Mix the flour and salt together in a bowl. Cut the fat (which should be quite firm) into cubes about 2 cm ($\frac{3}{4}$ inch) across.

2 Stir the fat into the flour without breaking up the pieces. Add enough water and lemon juice to mix to a fairly stiff dough.

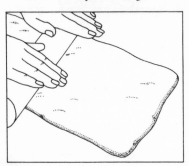

3 On a lightly floured surface, roll out into an oblong three times as long as it is wide.

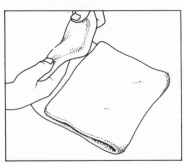

4 Fold the bottom third up and the top third down, then turn the pastry so that the folded edges are at the sides. Seal the ends of the pastry by pressing lightly with a rolling pin.

5 Repeat this rolling and folding process three more times, turning the dough so that the folded edge is on the left hand side each time.

6 Wrap the pastry in greaseproof paper and leave to rest in the refrigerator or a cool place for about 30 minutes before using.

7 Roll out the pastry on a lightly floured surface to 0.3 cm ($\frac{1}{8}$ inch) thick and use as required. Brush with beaten egg before baking. The usual oven temperature is 220°C (425°F) mark 7.

PUFF PASTRY

450 g (1 lb) strong plain flour
pinch of salt
450 g (1 lb) butter
about 300 ml ($\frac{1}{2}$ pint) cold water
15 ml (1 tbsp) lemon juice
beaten egg, to glaze

1 Mix the strong plain flour and a pinch of salt together in a large mixing bowl.

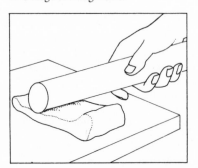

2 Cut off 50 g (2 oz) butter and pat the remaining butter with a rolling pin to a slab 2 cm ($\frac{3}{4}$ inch) thick.

3 Rub the 50 g (2 oz) butter into the flour with the finger and thumb tips. Stir in enough water and lemon juice to make a soft, elastic dough.

4 Knead dough until smooth and shape into a round. Cut through half the depth in a cross shape.

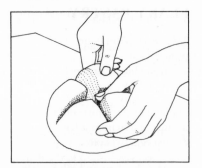

5 Open out the flaps to form a star. Roll out, keeping the centre four times as thick as the flaps.

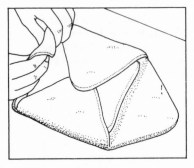

6 Place the slab of butter in the centre of the dough and fold over the flaps, envelope-style. Press gently with a rolling pin.

7 Roll out into a rectangle measuring about 40 × 20 cm (16 × 8 inches). Fold the bottom third up and the top third down, keeping the edges straight. Seal the edges by pressing with the rolling pin.

8 Wrap the pastry in greaseproof paper and leave in the refrigerator to rest for 30 minutes.

9 Put the pastry on a lightly floured working surface with the folded edges to the sides and repeat the rolling, folding and resting sequence five times.

10 After the final resting, roll out the pastry on a lightly floured surface and shape as required. Brush with beaten egg. The usual oven temperature is 230°C (450°F) mark 8.

FLAKY PASTRY

225 g (8 oz) plain flour
pinch of salt
75 g (3 oz) butter or block
   margarine
75 g (3 oz) lard
about 150 ml ($\frac{1}{4}$ pint) cold water
a squeeze of lemon juice
beaten egg, to glaze

1 Mix the flour and salt together in a bowl. Soften the fat by working it with a knife on a plate, then divide it into four equal portions.

2 Add one quarter of the fat to the flour and rub it in between finger and thumb tips until the mixture resembles fine breadcrumbs.

3 Add enough water and lemon juice to make a soft elastic dough, stirring it in with a round-bladed knife.

4 Turn the dough on to a lightly floured surface and roll out in to an oblong three times as long as it is wide.

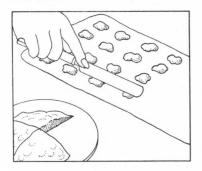

5 Using a round-bladed knife, dot another quarter of the fat over the top two-thirds of the pastry in flakes, so that it looks like buttons on a card.

6 Fold the bottom third of the pastry up and the top third down and turn it so that the folded edges are at the side. Seal the edges of the pastry by pressing with a rolling pin.

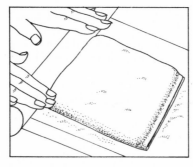

7 Re-roll as before and repeat the process twice more until the remaining portions of fat have been used up.

8 Wrap the pastry loosely in greaseproof paper and leave it to rest in the refrigerator or a cool place for at least 30 minutes before using.

9 Roll out the pastry on a lightly floured working surface to 0.3 cm ($\frac{1}{8}$ inch) thick and use as required. Brush with beaten egg before baking to give the characteristic glaze. When cooking flaky pastry, the usual oven temperature is 220°C (425°) mark 7.

CHOUX PASTRY

50 g (2 oz) butter or block
   margarine
150 ml ($\frac{1}{4}$ pint) water
65 g ($2\frac{1}{2}$ oz) plain flour, sifted
2 eggs, lightly beaten

BEATING CHOUX PASTRY

Add the beaten egg gradually to choux pastry, taking care to add only just enough to give a piping consistency. When beating by hand with a wooden spoon the arm tends to tire, the beating speed is reduced and the final consistency is often too slack to retain its shape. In this case a little less egg should be added. Use size 4 eggs if beating by hand and size 2 eggs when using an electric mixer.

1 Put the fat and water together in a pan, heat gently until the fat has melted, then bring to the boil. Remove pan from heat.

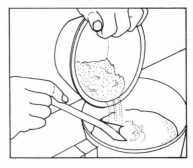

2 Tip all the flour at once into the hot liquid. Beat thoroughly with a wooden spoon, then return the pan to the heat.

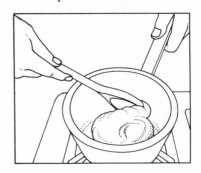

3 Continue beating the mixture until it is smooth and forms a ball in the centre of the pan. (Take care not to over-beat or the mixture will become fatty.) Remove from the heat and leave the mixture to cool for a minute or two.

4 Beat in the egg, a little at a time, adding only just enough to give a piping consistency. Beat the mixture vigorously at this stage to trap in as much air as possible. Continue beating until the mixture develops an obvious sheen, then use as required. When cooking choux pastry the usual oven temperature is 200–220°C (400–425°F) mark 6–7.

BISCUITS

Homemade biscuits beat bought ones any day, and they are so simple to make it is a pity to pass them by. Choose to make the thin and crisp type, or softer, thicker and more crumbly ones. They will all be equally popular.

The traditional biscuit mixture makes a dough that you roll out thinly and cut to shape before baking. If you find the dough sticky or difficult to handle, chill it a little, or roll it between sheets of non-stick parchment. Don't add extra flour to the working surface as this will spoil the texture of the biscuits.

Bar cookies are especially easy and quick to make. You mix the ingredients and press it all firmly into a baking tin. It is then cut into bars after baking.

Refrigerator biscuits are quick and easy to make. Make up the dough and shape it into a neat roll, then wrap it and place in the refrigerator or freezer. Then you just

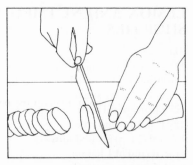

cut off thin slices, thaw slightly if frozen dough, and bake them, as and when you want freshly baked biscuits. The dough will keep quite happily for about 2 weeks in the refrigerator or 3 months in the freezer.

Dropped and piped recipes are a little more difficult to handle as the mixture is softer. These are either dropped from a spoon or piped on to baking sheets. They are inclined to spread, so leave plenty of space between each one.

Cook all biscuits on good-quality, flat baking sheets with no sides, to ensure even browning. Bake them in the centre of the oven, or if baking two sheets at a time, swap them over half way through. Leave soft cookies on the baking sheet for a few minutes after taking out of the oven, to firm up a little, then transfer carefully to a wire rack to cool.

Store biscuits in an airtight container. Most keep well for 2–3 weeks, but keep different varieties separate, so the flavours don't mix, and keep them separate from cakes. If you plan to ice biscuits, do it shortly before serving.

REFRIGERATOR BISCUITS

Makes 22

150 g (5 oz) caster sugar
150 g (5 oz) soft tub margarine
vanilla flavouring
grated rind of 1 lemon
1 egg, beaten
225 g (8 oz) plain flour

1 Cream together the sugar and margarine until very pale. Beat in a few drops of vanilla flavouring, the lemon rind and egg.

2 Stir in the flour and mix to a firm paste. Knead lightly, wrap and chill for 30 minutes.

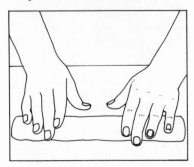

3 Roll the dough to a sausage shape, 5 cm (2 inches) in diameter, 20.5 cm (8 inches) long. Wrap in greaseproof paper. Refrigerate for at least 30 minutes before baking.

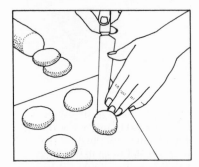

4 When required, cut 0.5-cm (¼-inch) slices, place on lightly greased baking sheets and bake in the oven at 190°C (375°F) mark 5 for 12–15 minutes. Cool on a wire rack.

FLAPJACKS

Makes 16–18

50 g (2 oz) butter or block margarine
50 g (2 oz) demerara sugar
45 ml (3 tbsp) golden syrup
100 g (4 oz) rolled oats

1 Grease an 18-cm (7-inch) square cake tin. Then melt the butter with the sugar and syrup, pour it on to the rolled oats and mix well.

2 Turn the mixture into the prepared tin and press down well. Bake in the oven at 180°C (350°F) mark 4 for 20–25 minutes until golden brown.

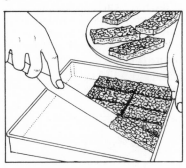

3 Cool slightly in the tin, mark into fingers with a sharp knife and loosen round the edges. When firm, cut right through and using a palette knife, remove the flapjacks from the tin.

LEMON AND NUTMEG SHORTIES

Makes 24

125 g (4 oz) butter or block margarine, softened
50 g (2 oz) caster sugar
175 g (6 oz) plain flour
25 g (1 oz) ground rice
1.25 ml ($\frac{1}{4}$ tsp) ground nutmeg
grated rind of 1 lemon
5 ml (1 tsp) lemon juice
caster sugar and nutmeg, to finish

1 Cream together the butter and sugar until very pale. Stir in the flour, ground rice, nutmeg, lemon rind and juice. Knead very well to form a smooth, workable paste.

2 On a lightly sugared surface, roll out the biscuit dough to slightly more than 0.5 cm ($\frac{1}{4}$ inch) thick.

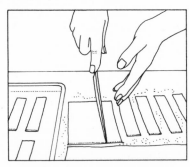

3 With a sharp knife, cut into 7.5 × 2 cm (3 × $\frac{3}{4}$ inch) fingers. Place on lightly greased baking sheets and chill for 30 minutes.

4 Bake in the oven at 190°C (375°F) mark 5 for about 25 minutes until just changing colour.

5 Dredge with caster sugar and ground nutmeg while still warm. Leave to cool completely on a wire rack.

CHERRY GARLANDS

Makes 24

225 g (8 oz) soft tub margarine
50 g (2 oz) icing sugar
200 g (7 oz) plain flour
150 g (5 oz) cornflour
vanilla flavouring
50 g (2 oz) glacé cherries, very finely chopped
whole cherries and angelica, to decorate
icing sugar

1 Cream the margarine and sugar together until pale and fluffy.

2 Beat in the flours, a few drops of vanilla flavouring and the chopped cherries. (If using an electric handmixer, beat for 3–4 minutes; by hand, beat until the mixture is very soft.)

3 Spoon half the mixture into a piping bag fitted with a 1-cm ($\frac{1}{2}$-inch) star nozzle. Pipe 5-cm (2-inch) rings on to lightly greased baking sheets allowing room for spreading.

4 Decorate with a quartered cherry and pieces of angelica. Repeat with the remaining mixture.

5 Bake in the oven at 190°C (375°F) mark 5 for about 20 minutes until pale golden. Allow to firm up slightly on the baking sheets for about 30 seconds before sliding on to a wire rack to cool. Dredge with icing sugar.

Decorating Cakes

'The icing on the cake' is the finishing touch that turns a workaday cake into a loving creation. Decorations for informal cakes may be anything from a light dusting of caster sugar or a smooth coat of glacé icing to whirls of butter cream interspersed with nuts or coloured sweets. For formal cakes you need to master piping techniques and the method of flat icing with royal icing.

EQUIPMENT

Simple decorations need no special equipment, but the right tools do help when you start to attempt more elaborate work.

An icing comb helps with icing the sides of a deep cake.

An icing nail is a small metal or polythene nail with a large head that is designed to hold decorations such as icing roses, while you make them. It enables you to hold the rose securely, and turn it without damaging it.

An icing ruler is useful for flat icing a large cake. You can substitute anything with a fine straight edge, long enough to extend both sides of the cake.

An icing turntable gives you clearance from the working surface and enables you to turn the cake freely. If you do not have a turntable, place the cake board on an upturned plate, to give it a little lift from the working surface.

Nozzles can be used with paper or fabric piping bags. A fine plain nozzle for writing and piping straight lines and simple designs, plus a star or shell nozzle, are the basics; more advanced piping work demands a whole range of different shapes and sizes. For use with paper piping bags, choose nozzles without a screw band; the band is useful with a fabric bag.

Piping bags can be made from greaseproof paper, or bought ready-made in fabric. Special icing pumps are also available.

A silver cake board or 'drum' sets off any iced cake. Some are made from thin card, or stronger ones are about 1 cm ($\frac{1}{2}$ inch) thick. Choose a board that is 5 cm (2 inches) larger than the cake, so that a border shows all round.

Apart from the above, the only tools you will need are everyday kitchen equipment: a palette knife, a table fork and a wire rack; for flat icing with royal icing you will need some fine sandpaper.

ICING

The cake must be completely cold before you start icing. The surface must be level; if necessary, turn the cake upside down and ice the flat bottom.

If making a sandwich or layer cake, put the filling in first. Then apply any decorations to the sides. Ice the top last.

For simple icings, place the cake on a wire rack to decorate it. Lifting it from one plate to another may crack the icing, and you are sure to make drips on the plate.

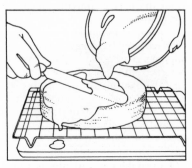

To use glacé icing, if coating both the top and sides of the cake, stand it on a wire rack with a tray underneath to catch the drips. As soon as the icing reaches a coating consistency and looks smooth and glossy, pour it from the bowl on to the centre of the cake. Allow the icing to run down the sides, guiding it with a palette knife. Keep a little icing back to fill the gaps.

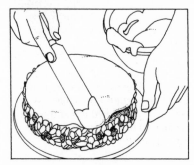

If the sides are decorated and only the top is to have glacé icing, pour the icing on to the centre of the cake and spread it with a palette knife, stopping just inside the edges to prevent it dripping down the sides. If the top is to be iced and the sides left plain, protect them with a band of greaseproof paper tied round the cake and projecting a little above it. Pour on the icing and let it find its own level. Peel off the paper when the icing is hard.

Arrange any ready-made decorations such as nuts, cherries, sweets, silver balls etc in position as soon as the icing has thickened and formed a skin. Except for feather icing, leave the icing until quite dry before applying piped decorations.

To feather ice, make a quantity of glacé icing (see page 154) and mix to a coating consistency. Make up a second batch of icing using half the quantity of sugar and enough warm water to mix it to a thick piping consistency; tint the second batch with food colouring. Spoon the coloured icing into a greaseproof paper piping bag.

Coat the top of the cake with the larger quantity of icing. Working quickly, before it has time to form a skin, snip the end off the piping bag and pipe parallel lines of coloured icing about 1–2 cm ($\frac{1}{2}$–$\frac{3}{4}$ inch) apart, over the surface. Then quickly draw the point of a skewer or a sharp knife across the piped lines, first in one direction then in the other, spacing them evenly apart.

Butter cream can be used as a filling or icing. Spread it over the top only, or over the top and sides. Decorate by making swirl marks

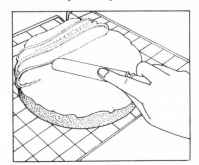

with the flat of a knife blade, or spread it evenly with a palette knife

and mark with the prongs of a fork. Add any extra decorations before it sets. For more elaborate decoration, butter cream pipes well.

Crème au beurre is a richer form of butter cream suitable for more elaborate cakes.

American frosting is a fluffy, soft icing. You need a sugar thermometer to make it. *Seven-minute frosting* is similar, but can be made without the help of a thermometer.

Almond paste is used on fruit cakes, either as a decoration in its own right, when it may be shaped and coloured as you wish, or as a firm base for royal icing.

Royal icing is the hard icing used on fruit cakes for formal occasions.

CAKE DECORATIONS

Add ready-made decorations before the icing hardens completely, or stick them in place with a little dab of fresh icing.

Nuts of all sorts, but particularly walnuts, hazelnuts, almonds and pistachios, are popular. Buy crystallised violets and roses in small quantities and keep them in a dark place to avoid bleaching. When buying angelica, look for a really good colour and a small amount of sugar. To remove sugar, soak briefly in hot water, then drain and dry well.

Chocolate and coloured vermicelli stale quickly and become speckled, so buy in small quantities as needed. Silver dragees (balls) keep well in a dry place; use tweezers for handling. They come in other colours than silver. Hundreds and thousands are useful for children's cakes, as are all sorts of coloured sweets, and for more sophisticated decorations, look for sugar coffee beans.

When decorating with chocolate, choose plain eating chocolate for chopping and grating. Chocolate-flavour cake covering is useful for scrolls and curls and also for melting, but the flavour is not so good. Crumbled chocolate flake makes a useful last minute decoration.

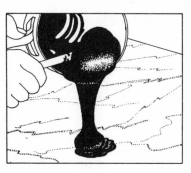

Chocolate caraque Melt 100 g (4 oz) chocolate in a bowl over a pan of hot water. Pour it in a thin layer on to a marble slab or cold baking tray and leave to set until it no longer sticks to your hand when you touch it. Holding a large knife with both hands, push the blade

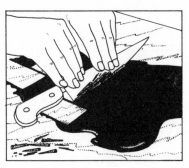

across the surface of the chocolate to roll pieces off in long curls. Adjust the angle of the blade to get the best curls.

Chocolate shapes Make a sheet of chocolate as above and cut into neat triangles or squares with a sharp knife, or stamp out circles with a small round cutter.

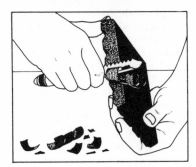

Chocolate curls Using a potato peeler, pare thin layers from the edge of a block of chocolate.

GLACÉ ICING

Makes about 100 g (4 oz)

100 g (4 oz) icing sugar

a few drops of vanilla or almond
  flavouring (optional)

15 ml (1 tbsp) warm water

colouring (optional)

1 Sift the icing sugar into a bowl.
  If you wish, add a few drops of
vanilla or almond flavouring.

2 Gradually add the warm water.
  The icing should be thick
enough to coat the back of a spoon.
If necessary add more water or
sugar to adjust consistency. Add
colouring, if liked, and use at once.

———— VARIATIONS ————

Orange or lemon Replace the
water with 15 ml (1 tbsp) strained
orange or lemon juice.
Chocolate Dissolve 10 ml (2 tsp)
cocoa powder in a little hot water
and use instead of the same amount
of water.
Coffee Flavour with 5 ml (1 tsp)
coffee essence or dissolve 10 ml
(2 tsp) instant coffee in a little
hot water and use instead of the
same amount of water.
Mocha Dissolve 5 ml (1 tsp) cocoa
powder and 10 ml (2 tsp) instant
coffee in a little hot water and use
instead of the same amount of
water.
Liqueur Replace 10–15 ml (2–3
tsp) of the water with the same
amount of any liqueur.

BUTTER CREAM

Makes 250 g (9 oz)

75 g (3 oz) butter

175 g (6 oz) icing sugar

a few drops of vanilla flavouring

15–30 ml (1–2 tbsp) milk or warm
  water

Put the butter in a bowl and cream
until soft. Gradually sift and beat
in the sugar, adding the vanilla
flavouring and milk or water.

———— VARIATIONS ————

Orange or lemon Replace the
vanilla flavouring with a little
finely grated orange or lemon rind.
Add a little juice from the fruit,
beating well to avoid curdling the
mixture.
Almond Add 30 ml (2 tbsp) finely
chopped toasted almonds and mix.
Coffee Replace the vanilla
flavouring with 10 ml (2 tsp) instant coffee blended with some of
the liquid, or replace 15 ml (1
tbsp) of the liquid with the same
amount of coffee essence.
Chocolate Dissolve 15 ml (1 tbsp)
cocoa powder in a little hot water
and cool before adding to the
mixture.
Mocha Dissolve 5 ml (1 tsp) cocoa
powder and 10 ml (2 tsp) instant
coffee in a little warm water taken
from the measured amount. Cool
before adding to the mixture.

APRICOT GLAZE

Makes 150 ml ($\frac{1}{4}$ pint)

100 g (4 oz) apricot jam

30 ml (2 tbsp) water

Put the jam and water in a saucepan and heat gently, stirring, until
the jam softens. Bring to the boil
and simmer for 1 minute. Sieve
the glaze and use while still warm.

CRÈME AU BEURRE
(Rich Butter Cream)

Makes about 275 g (10 oz)

75 g (3 oz) caster sugar

60 ml (4 tbsp) water

2 egg yolks, beaten

175 g (6 oz) butter

1 Place the sugar in a heavy
  based saucepan, add the water
and heat very gently to dissolve
the sugar, without boiling.

2 When completely dissolved,
  bring to boiling point and boil
steadily for 2–3 minutes, to reach
a temperature of 107°C (225°F).

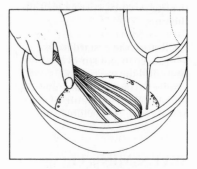

3 Pour the syrup in a thin
  stream on to the egg yolks in a
deep bowl, whisking all the time.
Continue to whisk until the mixture is thick and cold.

4 In another bowl, cream the
  butter until very soft and
gradually beat in the egg yolk
mixture.

———— VARIATIONS ————

Chocolate Melt 50 g (2 oz) plain
chocolate with 15 ml (1 tbsp)
water. Cool slightly and beat in.
Coffee Beat in 15–30 ml (1–2
tbsp) coffee essence.
Fruit Crush 225 g (8 oz) fresh
strawberries, raspberries etc, or
thaw, drain and crush frozen fruit.
Beat into the basic mixture.
Orange or lemon Add freshly
grated rind and juice to taste.

CREMÈ PATISSIÈRE

Makes 300 ml (½ pint)

2 eggs

50 g (2 oz) caster sugar

30 ml (2 tbsp) plain flour

30 ml (2 tbsp) cornflour

300 ml (½ pint) milk

a few drops of vanilla flavouring

1 Cream the eggs and sugar together until really pale and thick. Sift the flour and cornflour in to the bowl and beat in with a little cold milk until smooth.

2 Heat the rest of the milk until almost boiling and pour on to the egg mixture, stirring well all the time.

3 Return the custard to the saucepan and stir over a low heat until the mixture boils. Add vanilla flavouring to taste and cook for a further 2–3 minutes. Cover and allow to cool before using.

SEVEN-MINUTE FROSTING

Makes about 175 g (6 oz)

1 egg white

175 g (6 oz) caster sugar

pinch of salt

pinch of cream of tartar

30 ml (2 tbsp) water

1 Put all the ingredients into a bowl and whisk lightly. Then place the bowl over a pan of hot water and heat, whisking continuously, until the mixture thickens sufficiently to stand in peaks. This will take about 7 minutes depending on the whisk used and the heat of the water.

2 Pour the frosting over the top of the cake and spread with a palette knife.

—————— VARIATIONS ——————

Use the same flavourings as for American frosting.

ROYAL ICING

Makes about 900 g (2 lb)

4 egg whites

900 g (2 lb) icing sugar

15 ml (1 tbsp) lemon juice

10 ml (2 tbsp) glycerine

1 Whisk the egg whites in a bowl until slightly frothy. Then sift and stir in about a quarter of the icing sugar with a wooden spoon. Continue adding more sugar gradually, beating well after each addition, until about three quarters of the sugar has been added.

2 Beat in the lemon juice and continue beating for about 10 minutes until the icing is smooth.

3 Beat in the remaining sugar until the required consistency is achieved, depending on how the icing will be used.

4 Finally, stir in the glycerine to prevent the icing hardening. Cover and keep for 24 hours to allow air bubbles to rise to the surface.

ALMOND PASTE

Makes 900 g (2 lb)

225 g (8 oz) icing sugar

225 g (8 oz) caster sugar

450 g (1 lb) ground almonds

5 ml (1 tsp) vanilla flavouring

2 eggs, lightly beaten

10 ml (2 tsp) lemon juice

1 Sift the icing sugar into a bowl and mix in the caster sugar and ground almonds.

2 Add the vanilla flavouring, egg and lemon juice and mix to a stiff dough. Knead lightly and into a ball.

AMERICAN FROSTING

Makes about 225 g (8 oz)

1 egg white

225 g (8 oz) caster or granulated sugar

60 ml (4 tbsp) water

pinch of cream of tartar

1 Whisk the egg white until stiff. Then gently heat the sugar with the water and cream of tartar, stirring until dissolved. Then, without stirring, boil to 120°C (240°F).

2 Remove the syrup from the heat and, immediately the bubbles subside, pour it on to the egg white in a thin stream, beating the mixture continuously.

3 When it thickens, shows signs of going dull round the edges and is almost cold, pour the frosting quickly over the cake and spread evenly with a palette knife.

—————— VARIATIONS ——————

Orange Beat in a few drops of orange essence and a little orange food colouring before it thickens.
Lemon Beat in a little lemon juice before the mixture thickens.
Caramel Substitute demerara sugar for the white sugar.
Coffee Beat in 5 ml (1 tsp) coffee essence before mixture thickens.

CHOCOLATE FROSTING

Makes about 200 g (7 oz)

25 g (1 oz) plain chocolate

150 g (5 oz) icing sugar

1 egg

2.5 ml (½ tsp) vanilla flavouring

25 g (1 oz) butter

1 Break the chocolate into pieces and put in a bowl over a pan of hot water. Heat gently, stirring, until the chocolate has melted.

2 Sift in the icing sugar, add the egg, vanilla flavouring and butter and beat until smooth.

APPLYING ALMOND PASTE

Measure round the cake with a piece of string. Dust the working surface with icing sugar and roll out two-thirds of the paste to a rectangle, half the length of the string by twice the depth of the

cake. Trim the edges, then cut in half lengthways with a sharp knife.

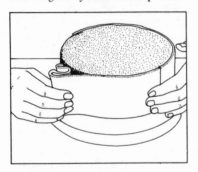

Place the cake upside down on a board and brush the sides with apricot glaze. Gently lift the almond paste and place it firmly in position round the cake.

Smooth the joins with a palette knife and keep the top and bottom edges square. Roll a jam jar lightly round the cake to help the paste stick more firmly.

Brush the top of the cake with apricot glaze and roll out the remaining almond paste to fit. With the help of the rolling pin, lift it

carefully on to the cake. Lightly roll with the rolling pin, then smooth the join and leave to dry for 2–5 days before starting to ice.

FLAT ICING WITH ROYAL ICING

Always apply royal icing over a layer of almond paste rather than directly on to the cake. Spoon almost half the icing on to the top of the cake and spread it evenly with a palette knife, using a paddling action to remove any air bubbles that may remain. Using an icing ruler or palette knife longer than the width of the cake, without

applying any pressure, draw it steadily across the top of the cake at an angle of 30°. Neaten the edges with a palette knife. Leave to dry for 24 hours before icing the sides.

To ice the sides, place the board on an icing turntable or on an upturned plate. Spread the remaining icing on the side of the cake and smooth it roughly with a small palette knife. Hold the palette knife or an icing comb upright and at an angle of 45° to the cake.

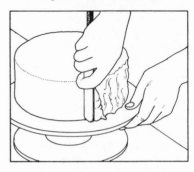

Draw the knife or comb towards you to smooth the surface. For a square cake, apply icing to each side separately. Reserve the surplus icing for decorating.

For a really smooth finish, allow to dry for 1–2 days then apply a second thinner coat of icing. Use fine sandpaper to sand down any imperfections in the first coat. Allow to dry thoroughly before adding piped decorations.

ICING AND ALMOND PASTE QUANTITIES

The amounts of almond paste quoted in this chart will give a thin covering. The quantities of royal icing should be enough for two coats.

Square tin size		15 cm (6 inches) square	18 cm (7 inches) square	20.5 cm (8 inches) square	23 cm (9 inches) square	25.5 cm (10 inches) square	28 cm (11 inches) square	30.5 cm (12 inches) square
Round tin size	15 cm (6 inches) round	18 cm (7 inches) round	20.5 cm (8 inches) round	23 cm (9 inches) round	25.5 cm (10 inches) round	28 cm (11 inches) round	30.5 cm (12 inches) round	
Almond paste	350 g (12 oz)	450 g (1 lb)	550 g (1¼ lb)	800 g (1¾ lb)	900 g (2 lb)	1 kg (2¼ lb)	1.1 kg (2½ lb)	1.4 kg (3 lb)
Royal icing	450 g (1 lb)	550 g (1¼ lb)	700 g (1½ lb)	900 g (2 lb)	1 kg (2¼ lb)	1.1 kg (2½ lb)	1.4 kg (3 lb)	1.6 kg (3½ lb)

PIPING

Butter cream, *crème au beurre*, stiff glacé icing and royal icing can all be piped. It is usual to pipe on to a base of the same kind of icing, though butter cream is sometimes piped on to glacé icing.

The icing used for piping must be completely free of lumps, or it will block the nozzle. It must also be exactly the right consistency to force easily through the nozzle, but still retain its shape.

Work with a small quantity at a time, refilling the piping bag frequently if necessary. If you are a beginner, practise on an upturned plate first. The practice icing can be scraped up while still soft and reused. Even on the real cake, if the base icing is hard mistakes can be scraped off and corrected.

Making a piping bag Fold a 25.5-cm (10-inch) square of greaseproof paper diagonally in half, then roll into a cone. Fold the points inwards to secure them. To insert a nozzle, snip off the tip of the bag and drop in the nozzle before adding the icing. For a very fine line, just snip off the end of the bag and use without a nozzle.

USING A PIPING BAG
Never more than half-fill the bag. When using a paper piping bag, fold the top flap down, enclosing the front edge, until the bag is sealed and quite firm; twist a fabric bag firmly closed. To hold the bag, lay it across the palm of one hand; with a paper bag, place your thumb firmly over the top of the bag, grasp the rest with the other four fingers and apply a steady even pressure until icing starts to come out of the nozzle. With a fabric bag grasp the bag where it is twisted with thumb and first finger and apply pressure with the remaining fingers.

To pipe a straight line: Place the tip of the nozzle where the line is to start. Apply slight pressure to the bag; as the icing starts to come out of the nozzle, lift the bag about 2.5 cm (1 inch) from the surface. This allows even the shakiest of hands to pipe a straight line. Move your hand in the direction of the line, guiding it with the other hand if you want, allowing the icing to flow evenly. About 1 cm ($\frac{1}{2}$ inch) before the end of the line, stop squeezing the bag and gently lower the tip of the nozzle to the surface.

To pipe dots: Only a slight pressure on the piping bag is required. Place the tip of the nozzle on the surface and hold the bag almost upright. Squeeze the bag gently and at the same time lift the nozzle slightly. Stop squeezing, move the nozzle slightly in a gentle shaking action to avoid a 'tail', and lift the nozzle. Larger dots can be made by moving the nozzle in a small circle or by using a larger nozzle.

To pipe stars: Fit the bag with a star nozzle. Hold the bag upright and just above the surface of the cake. Squeeze the icing out. As soon as the star is formed, stop squeezing and lift the bag away sharply.

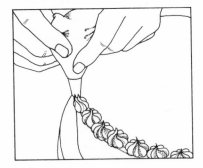

To pipe rosettes: Fit the bag with a star nozzle. Hold the icing bag upright, just above the surface of the cake. Squeeze gently and move the nozzle in a complete circle, filling in the centre. Pull the nozzle away sharply to avoid forming a point on the iced surface which would spoil the appearance of the piped rosette.

To pipe a shell border: Use either a star nozzle or a special shell nozzle; a shell nozzle will give a flatter, fuller shell with more ridges. In either case the movement is the same. Hold the bag at an angle to the surface and just above it. Squeeze until the icing begins to come from the nozzle and forms a head. Pull the bag gently and at the same time release

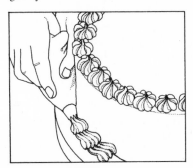

pressure to form the tail. Pipe the next shell just touching, and remember to release pressure each time to form the tail of the shell.

Writing: Use a plain writing nozzle and pipe as for a straight line (see left). Practise with simple capital letters at first. Before attempting to write on the cake, draw the letters on greaseproof paper and prick them on to the base icing with a pin; use the pin pricks as a guide. For fancier writing, magazines provide a useful source of stylised lettering.

To pipe a rose: Place a little icing on the top of an icing nail and stick a small square of non-stick paper on top. Fit the piping bag with a petal nozzle. Hold the bag with the thin part of the nozzle uppermost. Pipe a cone of icing, twisting the nail between thumb and finger, to form the centre of the rose. Pipe 5 or 6 petals around the centre, overlapping each petal and piping the outer ones so that they are more open, and lie flatter. Lift the square of paper from the nail and leave the rose uncovered for about 24 hours to dry. Attach it to the cake with a dab of icing.

DECORATING A CHRISTMAS CAKE

Christmas is a family occasion, so there's no need for an elaborate cake—keep it as simple as possible. Make the cake itself well in advance to give the flavour time to mature, and dose it with brandy from time to time.

Rough icing, to give the effect of snow, is a favourite choice for Christmas cakes, and the technique is simple enough even for a beginner—see the instructions for Festive Christmas Cake (right). Ready-made decorations such as Christmas trees and snowmen traditionally complete the picture, or you could make your own decorations: mould them from coloured almond paste, or shape them in tinted royal icing.

If you want something just a little more stylish try our Christmas Rosette Cake (right), decorated with ribbons and a candle.

Aim to complete the decorating about a week before Christmas. Once iced, the cake will keep fresh without an airtight tin, but protect it by covering it with a cake dome or an upturned box.

FESTIVE CHRISTMAS CAKE

Christmas cake (see page 90)
apricot glaze (see page 154)
550 g (1¼ lb) almond paste (see page 155)
700 g (1½ lb) royal icing (see page 155)
ribbon and Christmas cake decorations such as Santa Claus, snowmen, robins, reindeer or Christmas trees, to finish

1 14–20 days before required, place the cake on a 23-cm (9-inch) cake board. Brush with apricot glaze and cover with almond paste (see page 156). Loosely cover the cake and store in a cool dry place for 4–5 days.

2 Using the royal icing, roughly flat ice the top sides of the cake (see page 156). Leave to dry for 24 hours.

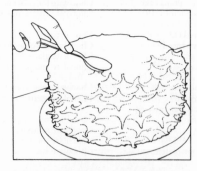

3 Spoon the remaining icing on top of the flat icing and roughly smooth it over with a palette knife. Using the palette knife or the back of a teaspoon, pull the icing in to well formed peaks.

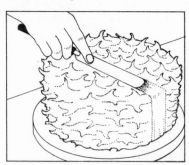

4 Using a palette knife, smooth a path down the centre of the top and side of the cake. Leave to dry for about 24 hours.

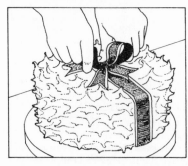

5 Place a piece of ribbon along the pathway, securing the ends with pins. Arrange the decorations on top, securing them if necessary with little dabs of fresh icing.

CHRISTMAS ROSETTE CAKE

Christmas cake (see page 90)
apricot glaze (see page 154)
550 g (1¼ lb) almond paste (see page 155)
700 g (1½ lb) royal icing (see page 155)
narrow red and green ribbons, a red candle and wide red ribbon, to finish

1 14–20 days before required, place the cake on a 23-cm (9-inch) cake board. Brush with apricot glaze and cover with almond paste (see page 156). Loosely cover the cake and store in a cool dry place for 4–5 days.

2 Using the royal icing, flat ice the top and sides of the cake. Leave to dry for about 24 hours.

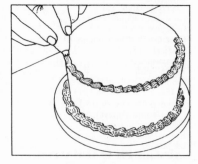

3 Using a piping bag fitted with an eight point star nozzle, pipe a shell border round the top edge. Pipe a shell border around the bottom edge.

4 Make a ribbon rosette with the narrow ribbons. Cut 3 longer pieces of green ribbon and 3 of red and arrange on top of the cake to form a star shape. Fix the ribbons and rosette in place with a little icing. Stand the candle firmly in the centre of the rosette. Place the wide ribbon round the cake and secure with a pin. Lay the narrow green ribbon over the wide ribbon, making sure it is central, then secure.

INDEX